The Observers Series

# AIRLINERS

## About the Book

*Observers Airliners* provides an invaluable pocket guide to the major types of aircraft used regularly by the world's airlines. Ninety different airliners are described and illustrated (with photographs and silhouettes throughout), ranging from the newest products of such giants as Boeing, British Aerospace and Airbus to the elderly but still useful classics such as the DC-3 and the Viscount. Here, too, will be found details of types yet to enter service when the book was published, among them a new generation of Soviet airliners being prepared for service in 1990. Important smaller types are included, too, although these have been restricted, in the main, to those used for regularly-scheduled services. Data have been corrected to the beginning of 1987.

## About the Authors

William Green, compiler of *Observers Aircraft* for 36 years, is internationally known for many works of aviation reference. William Green entered aviation journalism during the early years of World War II, subsequently served with the RAF and resumed aviation writing in 1947. He is currently managing editor of one of the largest circulation European-based aviation journals, *Air International*, and co-editor of *Air Enthusiast* and the *RAF Yearbook*.

Gordon Swanborough has spent virtually the whole of his working life as an aviation journalist and author, since joining Temple Press in 1943 on the staff of *The Aeroplane Spotter*. He is currently editor of *Air International* and co-editor, with William Green, of *Air Enthusiast* and *RAF Yearbook*, three publications that enjoy a world-wide reputation for authority and accuracy in the reporting of contemporary and historical aviation.

The *Observer's* series was launched in 1937 with the publication of *The Observer's Book of Birds*. Today, fifty years later, paperback *Observers* continue to offer practical, useful information on a wide range of subjects, and with every book regularly revised by experts, the facts are right up-to-date. Students, amateur enthusiasts and professional organisations alike will find the latest *Observers* invaluable.

'Thick and glossy, briskly informative' – *The Guardian*

'If you are a serious spotter of any of the things the series deals with, the books must be indispensable' – *The Times Educational Supplement*

O B S E R V E R S

# AIRLINERS

**William Green and Gordon Swanborough**

with silhouettes by Dennis Punnett

FREDERICK WARNE

FREDERICK WARNE
Penguin Books Ltd, Harmondsworth, Middlesex, England
Viking Penguin Inc., 40 West 23rd Street, New York, New York 10010, U.S.A.
Penguin Books Australia Ltd, Ringwood, Victoria, Australia
Penguin Books Canada Limited, 2801 John Street, Markham, Ontario, Canada L3R 1B4
Penguin Books (N.Z.) Ltd, 182–190 Wairau Road, Auckland 10, New Zealand

First published 1983
Reprinted 1984
Second edition 1987



ISBN 0 7232 3400 0

Typeset, printed and bound in Great Britain by
William Clowes Limited, Beccles and London

# INTRODUCTION

SINCE the first edition of *Observers Airliners* was published four years ago, in 1983, the airline business has gone through a period of considerable change. Worldwide economic factors served to depress air traffic growth in the early years of the present decade, leading many airlines to cut back on, or defer, their re-equipment plans. At the same time, deregulation in the USA—and moves towards similar 'economic regulatory reform' in Canada, Europe and elsewhere—served to change the pattern of the airline business to quite a fundamental degree. The result was to strengthen some airlines, to weaken others (to the point of bankruptcy in several cases) and, again, to cause variations in the numbers and types of new airliners being ordered.

All this made it difficult for the manufacturers to plan their future production programmes. While plans for new projects abounded, a secure financial basis on which to launch any brand new airliners remained elusive. Consequently, of the 16 aircraft in this edition that were not represented in the 1983 volume, 12 are variants of existing types—and of the four completely new aircraft included, two emanate from the Soviet Union.

Other factors than finance have also complicated the manufacturers' attempts to bring forward new designs. Falling oil prices, especially, reduced the pressure to achieve dramatic advances in fuel economy, and although direct operating costs remain significant for every airline, cheaper fuel has made it more difficult for the aircraft makers to show sufficient improvement to justify launching a new type instead of 'stretching' or otherwise improving an existing one. Hence the proliferation of Series or mark numbers to be found in this edition for types that were already established or were coming into production four years ago.

To make room for the new entries, some older and little-used types have been removed from this edition. Within the scope of 90 aircraft descriptions, it is also impossible to include most of the smaller (below 12 seats) types that operate in their hundreds at the bottom end of the air transport business—mostly on air taxi rather than scheduled airline duty. Also excluded are several new types that are the subject of intense marketing activity at the time this book goes to press, but none of which has yet become a firm programme—such as the Airbus A330 and A340, Boeing 7J7 and McDonnell Douglas MD-90 family. Some, at least, of these, are likely to go ahead and, when they do, they will introduce to commercial aviation the prop-fan engine—a concept that marries the best features of the turbofan and turboprop engines to offer exceptional economy of operation. The prop-fan is among the most exciting of aerospace developments of the 'eighties, and appears certain to feature as the power plant of at least one airliner to be described in the *third* edition of this title.

WG/FGS

# INTERNATIONAL CIVIL AIRCRAFT MARKINGS, BY COUNTRY

| | |
|---|---|
| Afghanistan | YA |
| Albania | ZA |
| Algeria | 7T |
| Andorra | C3 |
| Angola | D2 |
| Antigua | V2 |
| Argentina | LV |
| Australia | VH |
| Austria | OE |
| Bahamas | C6 |
| Bahrain | A9 |
| Bangladesh | S2 |
| Barbados | 8P |
| Belgium | OO |
| Belize | V3 |
| Benin | TY |
| Bermuda | VR-B |
| Bhutan | A5 |
| Bolivia | CP |
| Botswana | A2 |
| Bourkina Faso | XT |
| Brazil | PP & PT |
| British Virgin Islands | VP-LVA/LZZ |
| Brunei | V8 |
| Bulgaria | LZ |
| Burma | XY |
| Burundi | 9U |
| Cambodia (Kampuchea) | XU |
| Cameroon | TJ |
| Canada | C |
| Cape Verde Islands | D4 |
| Cayman Islands | VR-C |
| Central African Republic | TL |
| Chad | TT |
| Chile | CC |
| China (People's Republic) | B |
| Colombia | HK |
| Comoros Republic | D6 |
| Congo (Brazzaville) | TN |
| Costa Rica | TI |
| Cuba | CU |
| Cyprus | 5B |
| Czechoslovakia | OK |
| Denmark | OY |
| Djibouti | J2 |
| Dominica | J7 |
| Dominican Republic | HI |
| Ecuador | HC |
| Egypt | SU |
| Eire | EI, EJ |
| El Salvador | YS |
| Equatorial Guinea | 3C |
| Ethiopia | ET |
| Falkland Islands | VP-F |
| Fiji | DQ |
| Finland | OH |
| France | F |
| French Overseas Departments/ Protectorates | F-O |
| Gabon | TR |
| Gambia | C5 |
| Germany (Federal Republic) | D |
| Germany (GDR) | DDR |
| Ghana | 9G |
| Gibraltar | VR-G |
| Greece | SX |
| Grenada | J3 |
| Guatemala | TG |
| Guinea | 3X |
| Guinea/Bissau | J5 |
| Guyana | 8R |
| Haiti | HH |
| Honduras | HR |
| Hong Kong | VR-H |
| Hungary | HA |
| Iceland | TF |
| India | VT |
| Indonesia | PK |
| Iran | EP |
| Iraq | YI |
| Ireland | EI, EJ |
| Israel | 4X |
| Italy | I |
| Ivory Coast | TU |
| Jamaica | 6Y |
| Japan | JA |
| Jordan | JY |
| Kampuchea (Cambodia) | XU |
| Kenya | 5Y |
| Kiribati | T3 |
| Korea (Democratic People's Republic) | P |
| Korea (Republic of) | HL |
| Kuwait | 9K |
| Laos | RDPL |
| Lebanon | OD |
| Lesotho | 7P |
| Liberia | EL |
| Libya | 5A |
| Liechtenstein | HB |
| Luxembourg | LX |
| Madagascar | 5R |
| Malawi | 7Q |
| Malaysia | 9M |

|  |  |
|---|---|
| Maldive Republic | 8Q |
| Mali | TZ |
| Malta | 9H |
| Mauritania | 5T |
| Mauritius | 3B |
| Mexico | XA, XB, XC |
| Monaco | 3A |
| Mongolia | HMAY |
| Montserrat | VP-LMA/LUZ |
| Morocco | CN |
| Mozambique | C9 |
| Namibia | ZS |
| Nauru | C2 |
| Nepal | 9N |
| Netherlands | PH |
| Netherlands Antilles | PJ |
| New Zealand | ZK, ZL, ZM |
| Nicaragua | YN |
| Niger | 5U |
| Nigeria | 5N |
| Norway | LN |
| Oman | A40 |
| Pakistan | AP |
| Panama | HP |
| Papua New Guinea | P2 |
| Paraguay | ZP |
| Peru | OB |
| Philippines | RP |
| Poland | SP |
| Portugal | CS |
| Puerto Rico | N |
| Qatar | A7 |
| Romania | YR |
| Rwanda | 9XR |
| St Kitts-Nevis | VP-LKA/LLZ |
| St Lucia | J6 |
| St Vincent and Grenadines | J8 |
| Samoa (Western) | 5W |
| São Tome Island | S9 |
| Saudi Arabia | HZ |
| Senegal | 6V |
| Seychelles | S7 |
| Sierre Leone | 9L |
| Singapore | 9V |
| Solomon Islands | H4 |
| Somalia | 6O |
| South Africa | ZS, ZT, ZU |
| Soviet Union | CCCP |
| Spain | EC |
| Sri Lanka | 4R |
| Sudan | ST |
| Surinam | PZ |
| Swaziland | 3D |
| Sweden | SE |
| Switzerland | HB |
| Syria | YK |
| Taiwan (Republic of China) | B |
| Tanzania | 5H |
| Thailand | HS |
| Togo | 5V |
| Tonga Friendly Islands | A3 |
| Transkei | ZS |
| Trinidad & Tobago | 9Y |
| Tunisia | TS |
| Turkey | TC |
| Turks and Caicos Islands | VQ-T |
| Tuvalu | T3 |
| Uganda | 5X |
| United Arab Emirates | A6 |
| United Kingdom | G |
| Uruguay | CX |
| USA (and outlying territories) | N |
| Vanuatu | YJ |
| Venezuela | YV |
| Vietnam | XV, VN |
| Virgin Islands (British) | VP-LVA/LZZ |
| Western Samoa | 5W |
| Yemen (Arab Republic) | 4W |
| Yemen (People's Democratic Republic) | 7O |
| Yugoslavia | YU |
| Zaire | 9Q |
| Zambia | 9J |
| Zimbabwe | Z |

# INTERNATIONAL CIVIL AIRCRAFT MARKINGS, BY DESIGNATOR

| | |
|---|---|
| AP | Pakistan |
| A2 | Botswana |
| A3 | Tonga Friendly Islands |
| A5 | Bhutan |
| A6 | United Arab Emirates |
| A7 | Qatar |
| A9 | Bahrain |
| A40 | Oman |
| B | China (People's Republic) |
| B | China/Taiwan (R o C) |
| C | Canada |
| CC | Chile |
| CCCP | Soviet Union |
| CN | Morocco |
| CP | Bolivia |
| CS | Portugal |
| CU | Cuba |
| CX | Uruguay |
| C2 | Naura |
| C3 | Andorra |
| C5 | Gambia |
| C6 | Bahamas |
| C9 | Mozambique |
| D | Federal Republic of Germany |
| DDR | German Democratic Republic |
| DQ | Fiji |
| D2 | Angola |
| D4 | Cape Verde Republic |
| D6 | Comoro Republic |
| EC | Spain |
| EI, EJ | Eire |
| EL | Liberia |
| EP | Iran |
| ET | Ethiopia |
| F | France |
| F-O | French Overseas Departments/ Protectorates |
| G | United Kingdom |
| HA | Hungary |
| HB | Switzerland & Liechtenstein |
| HC | Ecuador |
| HH | Haiti |
| HI | Dominican Republic |
| HK | Colombia |
| HL | Republic of Korea |
| HMAY | Mongolia |
| HP | Panama |
| HR | Honduras |
| HS | Thailand |
| HZ | Saudi Arabia |
| H4 | Solomon Islands |
| I | Italy |
| JA | Japan |
| JY | Jordan |
| J2 | Djibouti |
| J3 | Grenada |
| J5 | Guinea Bissau |
| J6 | St Lucia |
| J7 | Dominica |
| J8 | St Vincent and Grenadines |
| LN | Norway |
| LV | Argentina |
| LX | Luxembourg |
| LZ | Bulgaria |
| MI | Marshall Islands |
| N | USA |
| OB | Peru |
| OD | Lebanon |
| OE | Austria |
| OH | Finland |
| OK | Czechoslovakia |
| OO | Belgium |
| OY | Denmark |
| P | Korea |
| PH | Netherlands |
| PJ | Netherlands Antilles |
| PK | Indonesia |
| PP, PT | Brazil |
| PZ | Surinam |
| P2 | Papua New Guinea |
| RDPL | Laos |
| RP | Philippines |
| SE | Sweden |
| SP | Poland |
| ST | Sudan |
| SU | Egypt |
| SX | Greece |
| S2 | Bangladesh |
| S7 | Seychelles |
| S9 | São Tome Islands |
| TC | Turkey |
| TF | Iceland |
| TG | Guatemala |
| TI | Costa Rica |
| TJ | Cameroon |
| TL | Central African Republic |
| TN | Congo Brazzaville |
| TR | Gabon |
| TS | Tunisia |
| TT | Chad |
| TU | Ivory Coast |
| TY | Benin |
| TZ | Mali |

| | |
|---|---|
| T3 | Kiribati |
| VH | Australia |
| VN | Vietnam |
| VP-F | Falkland Islands |
| VP-H | Belize |
| VP-LKA/LLZ | St Kitts-Nevis-Anguilla |
| VP-LMA/LUZ | Montserrat |
| VP-LVA/LZZ | British Virgin Islands |
| VQ-T | Turks & Caicos Islands |
| VR-B | Bermuda |
| VR-C | Cayman Islands |
| VR-G | Gibraltar |
| VR-H | Hong Kong |
| VT | India |
| V2 | Antigua |
| V3 | Belize |
| V8 | Brunei |
| XA, XB, XC | Mexico |
| XT | Bourkina Faso |
| XU | Cambodia |
| XV | Vietnam |
| XY | Burma |
| YA | Afghanistan |
| YI | Iraq |
| YJ | Vanuatu |
| YK | Syria |
| YN | Nicaragua |
| YR | Romania |
| YS | El Salvador |
| YU | Yugoslavia |
| YV | Venezuela |
| Z | Zimbabwe |
| ZA | Albania |
| ZK, ZL, ZM | New Zealand |
| ZP | Paraguay |
| ZS, ZT, ZU | South Africa |
| 3A | Monaco |
| 3B | Mauritius |
| 3C | Equatorial Guinea |
| 3D | Swaziland |
| 3X | Guinea |
| 4R | Sri Lanka |
| 4W | Yemen Arab Republic |
| 4X | Israel |
| 5A | Libya |
| 5B | Cyprus |
| 5H | Tanzania |
| 5N | Nigeria |
| 5R | Malagasy Republic |
| 5T | Mauritania |
| 5U | Niger |
| 5V | Togo |
| 5W | Western Samoa |
| 5X | Uganda |
| 5Y | Kenya |
| 6O | Somalia |
| 6V | Senegal |
| 6Y | Jamaica |
| 7O | People's Dem. Rep. of Yemen |
| 7P | Lesotho |
| 7Q | Malawi |
| 7T | Algeria |
| 8P | Barbados |
| 8Q | Maldive Republic |
| 8R | Guyana |
| 9G | Ghana |
| 9H | Malta |
| 9J | Zambia |
| 9K | Kuwait |
| 9L | Sierra Leone |
| 9M | Malaysia |
| 9N | Nepal |
| 9Q | Zaïre |
| 9U | Burundi |
| 9V | Singapore |
| 9XR | Rwanda |
| 9Y | Trinidad & Tobago |

## AUTHORS' ACKNOWLEDGEMENT

The authors wish to thank the public relations staffs of the principal manufacturers whose products are represented in this book, for assistance with data and photographs. Grateful acknowledgement is also made to the several individuals who have provided photographs.

## AEROSPATIALE CARAVELLE

**Country of Origin:** France
**Type:** Short-to-medium-range jet transport.
**Power Plant:** (Caravelle 10B): Two 14,500 lb st (6 580 kgp) Pratt & Whitney JT8D-9 turbofans.
**Performance:** (Caravelle 10B): Max cruising speed, 445 kts (825 km/h) at 25,000 ft (7 620 m); range with max payload, 1,450 naut mls (2 650 km); range with max fuel, 1,965 naut mls (3 640 km).
**Accommodation:** Flight crew of three and up to 110 passengers five-abreast with one aisle at 29-in (74-cm) pitch; typical mixed-class layout for 91.
**Status:** Prototypes first flown on 25 May 1955 and 6 May 1956; certification 2 April 1958; first production Caravelle I flown 18 May 1958 and first service (Air France) flown on 6 May 1959. First flights of later variants: Caravelle IA, 11 February 1960; III, 30 December 1959; VI-N, 10 September 1960; VI-R, 6 February 1961; VII, 29 December 1960; 10A, 31 August 1962; 10B/Super B, 3 March 1964; 10R, 18 January 1965; 11R, 21 April 1967; 12, 29 October 1970. Production ended 1972.
**Sales:** Production total 282, including three prototypes; 20 Caravelle I; 12 IA; 78 III; 53 VI-N; 56 VI-R; one VII; one 10A; 22 10B; 20 10R; six 11R; 12 Super Caravelle 12.
**Notes:** Caravelle Mks I, IA, III and VI had same overall dimensions, different engine versions and weights. Caravelle Mks VII, 10, 11 and 12 featured JT8D engines in place of original Rolls-Royce Avons, and the Caravelle 11 and 12 introduced fuselage stretches of 3 ft 0½ in (0.93 m) and 10 ft 7 in (3.21 m) respectively. About 70 Caravelles of assorted type were in airline service in 1986, particularly with charter airlines in Europe.

## AEROSPATIALE CARAVELLE 10B

**Dimensions:** Span, 112 ft 6 in (34,30 m); length, 108 ft $3\frac{1}{2}$ in (33,01 m); height, 28 ft 7 in (8,72 m); wing area, 1,579 sq ft (146,7 m²).
**Weights:** Operating weight empty, 66,260 lb (30 055 kg); max payload, 20,060 lb (9 100 kg); max take-off, 123,460 lb (56 000 kg); max landing, 109,130 lb (49 500 kg).

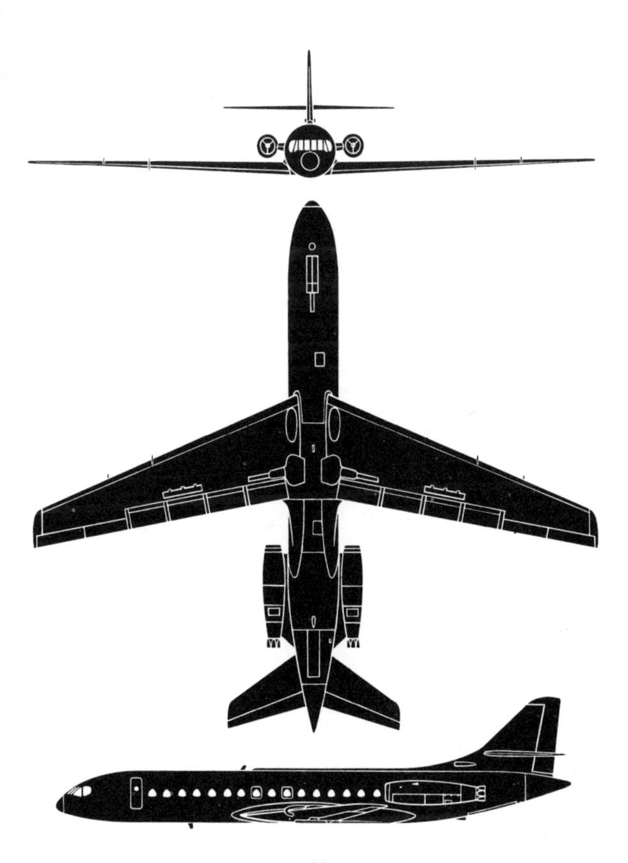

## AEROSPATIALE (NORD) 262 FREGATE

**Country of Origin:** France.
**Type:** Short-range turboprop transport.
**Power Plant:** (N262C): Two 1,130 shp (843 kW) Turboméca Bastan VIIC turboprops.
**Performance:** (N262C): Max cruise, 225 kts (415 km/h) at 20,000 ft (6 100 m); range with max payload (26 passengers), 565 mls (915 km); range with max fuel, 985 naut mls (1 825 km).
**Accommodation:** Flight crew of two and up to 29 passengers, three-abreast with offset aisle at 33-in (84-cm) seat pitch.
**Status:** MH-250 prototype flown 20 May 1959; MH-260 prototype flown 29 July 1960; Nord 262 prototype flown 24 December 1962, certificated 16 July 1964. First production (262B) flown 8 July 1964, first 262A flown early 1965, certificated March, entered service August. N262C flown July 1968 and certificated 24 December 1970. Mohawk 298 conversion flown 7 January 1975, certificated 19 October 1976. Production completed 1975.
**Sales:** Production total 110, including four N262B, 67 N262A and military orders for N262D Frégate.
**Notes:** The Nord 262 design was based on the original unpressurized Super Broussard project of the Max Holste company, which built one piston-engined MH-250 and a prototype plus 10 pre-production MH-260s with Bastan turboprops. Nord developed a pressurized circular-section fuselage for the N262, built in four variants, during which time the company merged with Sud to form Aérospatiale. In the USA, nine N262s were converted to Mohawk 298 standard with PT6A-45 engines and systems improvements, deriving this designation from FAR Part 298 airworthiness requirements. About 30 Nord 262s/ Mohawk 298s were in airline service at the end of 1986.

## AEROSPATIALE (NORD) 262C

**Dimensions:** Span, 74 ft 2 in (22,60 m); length, 63 ft 3 in (19,28 m); height, 20 ft 4 in (6,21 m); wing area, 592 sq ft (55,0 m$^2$).
**Weights:** Basic operating, 15,929 lb (7 225 kg); max payload, 6,781 lb (3 075 kg); max zero fuel, 22,710 lb (10 300 kg); max take-off, 23,810 lb (10 800 kg); max landing, 23,040 lb (10 450 kg).

## AEROSPATIALE/AERITALIA ATR 42

**Country of Origin:** France and Italy.
**Type:** Short-range regional airliner.
**Power Plant:** Two flat-rated 1,800 shp (1 342 kW) Pratt & Whitney PW120 turboprops.
**Performance:** (ATR 42-200): Max cruising speed, 268 kts (497 km/h) at 17,000 ft (5 180 m); range with max payload, 645 naut mls (1 195 km); range with max fuel, 2,490 naut mls (4 614 km).
**Accommodation:** Flight crew of two and up to 50 passengers four-abreast with single aisles at 30-in (76-cm) pitch; typical layout for 42 passengers.
**Status:** Two prototype/development aircraft, first flown 16 August and 31 October 1984. First production aircraft flown 30 April 1985. French certification of ATR 42–200 and ATR 42–300 on 24 September 1985, and first services flown by Air Littoral on 9 December. FAA certification on 25 October 1985 followed by deliveries to first US customer, Command Airways.
**Sales:** Total of 74 firm sales by early 1987 plus approximately 24 more on option.
**Notes:** Collaborative programme for this Avion de Transport Regional (hence ATR) between Aérospatiale (France) and Aeritalia (Italy) was launched in October 1981, with final assembly by former. The ATR 42–200 is the basic initial version. ATR 42–300 has same overall dimensions but operates at higher gross weight of 34,725 lb (15 750 kg) to carry bigger passenger payload in high-density layout. Freighter version is designated ATR 42-F. Stretched-fuselage ATR 72 is separately described on the next pages.

## AEROSPATIALE/AERITALIA ATR 42

**Dimensions:** Span, 80 ft 7½ in (24,57 m); length, 74 ft 4½ in (22,67 m); height, 24 ft 10¾ in (7,59 m); wing area, 586.6 sq ft (54,5 m²).
**Weights:** Operating weight empty, 21,986 lb (9 973 kg); max payload, 9,980 lb (4 527 kg); max fuel, 9,920 lb (4 500 kg); max take-off, 34,725 lb (15 750 kg); max landing, 34,171 lb (15 500 kg).

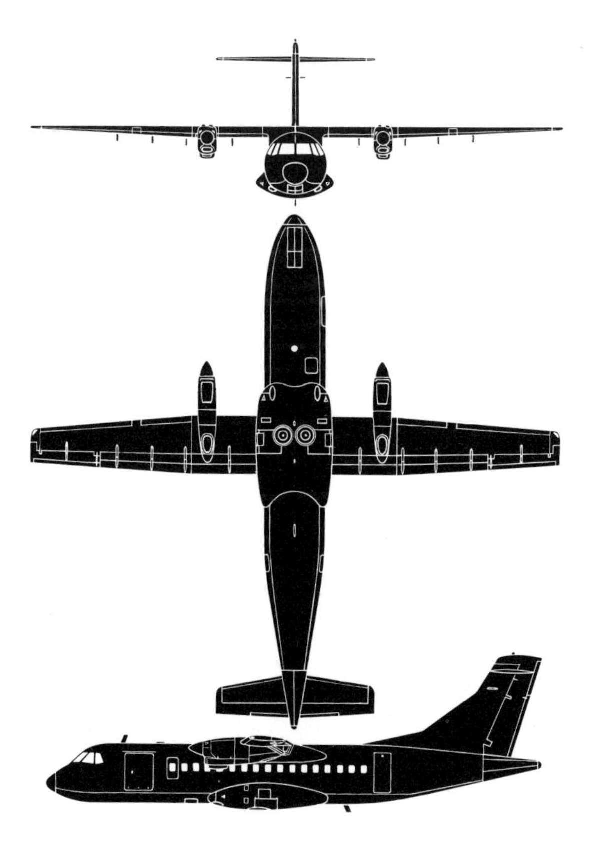

## AEROSPATIALE/AERITALIA ATR 72

**Country of Origin:** France and Italy.
**Type:** Short-to-medium range regional airliner.
**Power Plant:** Two flat-rated 2,400 shp (1 791 kW) Pratt & Whitney PW124 turboprops.
**Performance:** Max cruising speed, 286 kts (530 km/h); max operational cruise altitude, 25,000 ft (7 600 m); range with max payload, 700 naut mls (1 300 km); range with max fuel, and zero payload, 2,400 naut mls (4 447 km).
**Accommodation:** Flight crew of two and up to 74 passengers four-abreast with single aisle at 30-in (76-cm) pitch; typical layout for 66 passengers at 31-in (79-cm) pitch.
**Status:** Launched in 1985 as stretched derivative of ATR 42. First flight scheduled summer 1988; deliveries scheduled to begin 1989.
**Sales:** Total of 5 firm sales by early 1987, plus approximately 20 more on option.
**Notes:** The ATR 72 was developed as a straightforward stretch of the ATR 42 (see previous pages) to meet the projected needs of the regional airlines for an aircraft in the 60/70-seat category. A high degree of commonality with the ATR 42 makes the aircraft of particular interest to operators of the smaller type. The lengthening of the fuselage by 14 ft (4,27 m) allows for six more seat rows to bring the maximum accommodation to 74, and the wing span is extended by 8 ft $1\frac{1}{2}$ in (2,48 cm) to allow increased area to match the higher operating weights. A cargo door in the forward port side is optional, facilitating use of the ATR 72 in mixed-traffic or all-freight operations.

## AEROSPATIALE/AERITALIA ATR 72

**Dimensions:** Span, 88 ft 9 in (27,05 m); length 89 ft $1\frac{1}{2}$ in (27,17 m); height, 25 ft 1 in (7,65 m); wing area, 657 sq ft (61,0 $m^2$).
**Weights:** Operating weight empty, 26,895 lb (12 200 kg); max payload, 15,765 lb (7 150 kg); max fuel, 11,025 lb (5 000 kg); max take-off, 44,070 lb (19 990 kg); max landing, 43,870 lb (19 900 kg).

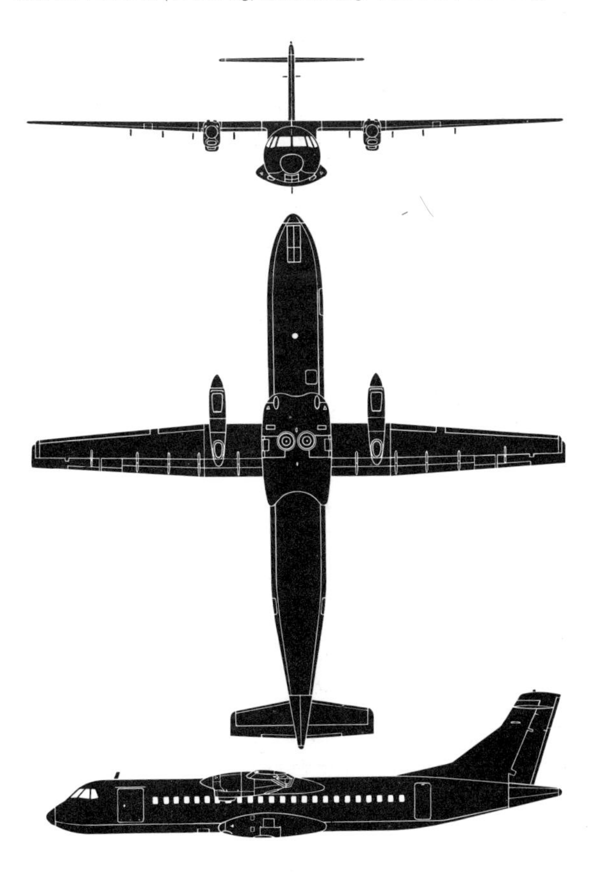

# AEROSPATIALE/BAe CONCORDE

**Country of Origin:** United Kingdom and France.
**Type:** Medium-range supersonic transport.
**Power Plant:** Four 38,050 lb st (17 260 kgp) Rolls-Royce (Bristol)/SNECMA Olympus 593 Mk 610 reheated turbojets.
**Performance:** Max cruise, 1,176 kts (2 179 km/h) at 51,300 ft (15 635 m); range with max payload, 3,360 naut mls (6 230 km); range with max fuel, 3,550 naut mls (6 580 km).
**Accommodation:** Flight crew of three and 128 passengers four abreast with central aisle at 34-in (86-cm) pitch; maximum, 144 passengers.
**Status:** Prototypes 001 and 002 first flown on 2 March 1969 (Toulouse) and 9 April 1969 (Filton); pre-production 01 and 02 first flown 17 December 1971 (Toulouse) and 10 January 1973 (Filton). First two production Concordes flown 6 December 1973 (Toulouse) and 13 February 1974 (Filton). Certification 13 October 1975 (France) and 5 December 1975 (UK); first revenue services 21 January 1976 (Air France and UK). Last production aircraft flown, 26 December 1978 (Toulouse) and 20 April 1979 (Filton).
**Sales:** Seven each to Air France and British Airways; first two production aircraft not brought up to full delivery standard.
**Notes:** Concorde is to date the only supersonic transport successfully put into airline service, although its operation has to be subsidized by British and French governments. Services have been flown on routes to the Middle and Far East and across the South Atlantic, but by 1983 the London and Paris routes to New York and Washington were the only ones flown regularly by the two airlines, with the BA route extended from Washington to Miami in March 1984. Charter flights take Concorde to many other parts of the world.

## AEROSPATIALE/BAe CONCORDE

**Dimensions:** Span, 83 ft 10 in (25,56 m); length, 203 ft 9 in (62,17 m); height, 37 ft 5 in (11,40 m); wing area, 3,856 sq ft (358,25 m$^2$).
**Weights:** Operating empty, 189,400 lb (85 900 kg); max payload, 28,000 lb (12 700 kg); max take-off, 408,000 lb (185 070 kg); max landing, 245,000 lb (111 130 kg).

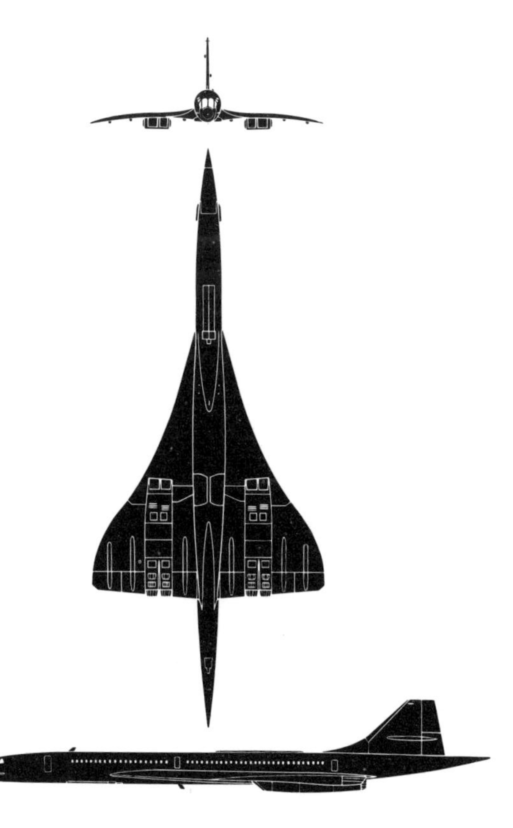

## AIRBUS A300-600

**Country of Origin:** International.

**Type:** Medium-to-long range large capacity transport.

**Power Plant:** Two 56,000 lb st (25 400 kgp) General Electric CF6-80C2 or Pratt & Whitney JT9D-7R4H1 or PW 4156 or 58,000 lb st (26 310 kgp) PW 4158 turbofans.

**Performance:** (A300-600, CF6-80C2 engines): Max cruising speed, 480 kts (891 km/h) at 31,000 ft (9 450 m); long-range cruising speed, 457 kts (847 km/h) at 35,000 ft (10 670 m); range with max payload, 2,310 naut mls (5 390 km); range with max fuel, 4,380 naut mls (8 120 km).

**Accommodation:** Flight crew of two and up to 375 passengers, six/seven/eight/nine-abreast with two aisles; typical mixed-class layout for 267—20 six-abreast and 247 eight-abreast.

**Status:** A300B1 prototypes flown on 28 October 1972 and 5 February 1973. First B2 flown 28 June 1973; certification, 15 March 1974; entry into service (Air France) 23 May 1974. First B4 flown 26 December 1974; first with JT9D engines flown 28 April 1979; first with FFCC flown 6 October 1981. A300-600 first flown 8 July 1983 with JT9D engines, certificated 9 March 1984; first A300-600 with CF6-80C2 engines flown 20 March 1985.

**Sales:** 279 firm orders, of which 270 delivered by end 1986.

**Notes:** The A300 is manufactured by a consortium of Aérospatiale (France), Deutsche Airbus (Germany) and British Aerospace (UK), with small shares held by Fokker (Netherlands) and CASA (Spain). The A300B4-100 is heavier longer-range version of original A300B2-100. B4-200 has further weight increase and A300-600 has redesigned rear fuselage, wing modifications and other improvements for improved economy and A300-600R in 1987 introduces a tailplane fuel tank, PW 4000 engine option, winglets and 375,880 lb (170 500 kg) gross weight. The A300C4 has a side-loading cargo door.

## AIRBUS A300-600

**Dimensions:** Span, 147 ft $1\frac{1}{2}$ in (44,84 m); length, 177 ft 5 in (54,08 m); height, 54 ft $6\frac{1}{2}$ in (16,62 m); wing area, 2,798.6 sq ft (260,0 m$^2$).

**Weights:** Operating weight empty, 197,787 lb (89 715 kg); max payload, 88,813 lb (40 285 kg); max fuel, 111,331 lb (50 499 kg); max take-off, 363,765 lb (165 000 kg); max landing, 304,240 lb (138 000 kg).

## AIRBUS A310-300

**Country of Origin:** International.
**Type:** Short-to-medium range large capacity transport.
**Power Plant:** Two 50,000 lb st (22 680 kgp) General Electric CF6-80C2 or Pratt & Whitney JT9D-7R4EI or PW 4150 turbofans.
**Performance** (A310-300, JT9D engines): Max cruising speed, 484 kts (897 km/h) at 35,000 ft (10 670 m); long-range best economy cruising speed, 463 kts (860 km/h) at 37,000 ft (11 280 m); range with max payload, 3,750 naut mls (6 950 km); range with max fuel, 5,240 naut mls (9 710 km).
**Accommodation:** Flight crew of two and up to 280 passengers nine-abreast with two aisles at 30-in (76-cm) pitch; typical mixed-class layout for 18 six-abreast and 200 eight-abreast.
**Status:** Three A310 development aircraft flown on 3 April, 13 May and 5 August 1982, comprising two -220 with JT9D engines and one -200 with CF6 engines. Certification, 11 March 1983, followed by service introduction by Swissair and Lufthansa on 12 and 21 April 1983 respectively. A310-300 first flown on 8 July 1985 (JT9D engines), 6 September 1985 (CF6-80 engines) and 8 November 1986 (PW4000 engines).
**Sales:** 130 firm orders by early 1987; over 90 delivered.
**Notes:** A310 is a reduced-capacity derivative of the A300, featuring a shortened fuselage, brand-new wing, updated systems and application of new materials where suitable. Basic aircraft is the A310-200 (CF6 engines) or -220 (JT9D engines); higher weight options of these are also on offer. The A310-300 carries an extra 15,430 lb (7 000 kg) of fuel in the tailplane to increase the range, and has a maximum take-off weight of 337,305 lb (153 000 kg). A310C convertible and A310F all-freight versions are available.

## AIRBUS A310-300

**Dimensions:** Span, 144 ft 0 in (43,90 m); length, 153 ft 1 in (46,66 m); height, 51 ft 10 in (15,81 m); wing area, 2,357 sq ft (219,0 m²).
**Weights:** Operating weight empty, 169,840 lb (77 040 kg); max payload, 75,400 lb (34 200 kg); max fuel, 109,023 lb (49 452 kg); max take-off, 337,305 lb (153 000 kg); max landing, 271,170 lb (123 000 kg).

## AIRBUS A320

**Country of Origin:** International.
**Type:** Short-to-medium range jet transport.
**Power Plant:** Two 23,500–25,000 lb st (10 660–11 340 kgp) CFM International CFM56-5 or International Aero Engines V2500 turbofans.
**Performance** (A320-100): Max cruising speed, 487 kts (903 km/h) at 28,000 ft (8 530 m); long-range cruising speed, 454 kts (840 km/h) at 37,000 ft (11 280 m); range with max payload, 1,860 naut mls (3 450 km); range with max fuel, 2,640 naut mls (4 830 km).
**Accommodation:** Flight crew of two and up to 179 passengers six-abreast with one aisle at 30-in (76-cm) pitch; typical mixed-class layout for 12 four-abreast and 138 six-abreast.
**Status:** First flight of Airbus A320 on 22 February 1987 with CFM56-5 engines. First airline deliveries, April 1988; production rate up to 5-6 a month by 1990.
**Sales:** Firm orders for 271 by early 1987, plus 166 options, from All Nippon, Air France, Air Inter, Aliã, Ansett, Australian, British Caledonian, Cyprus Airways, GATX, GPA Airbus 320, Indian Airlines, Inex Adria, Lufthansa, Northwest and Pan Am.
**Notes:** The A320 was launched into development and production in March 1984 when British and German financial participation was agreed by respective governments, to add to French government support already authorized. Major work shares are: Aérospatiale, 34 per cent, Deutsche Airbus 35 per cent, British Aerospaçe 24 per cent, CASA, 5 per cent and Belairbus (Belgium), 2 per cent. The A320-200 has a 158,700 lb (72 000 kg) gross weight.

## AIRBUS A320-100

**Dimensions:** Span, 111 ft 3 in (33,91 m); length, 123 ft 3 in (37,58 m); height, 38 ft 7 in (11,76 m); wing area, 1,317 sq ft (122,40 m²).
**Weights** (A320-100): Operating weight empty, 84,170 lb (38 180 kg); max payload, 41,530 lb (18 840 kg); max fuel, 27,200 lb (12 338 kg); max take-off, 145,500 lb (66 000 kg); max landing, 134,480 lb (61 000 kg).

# AIRTECH (CASA-IPTN) CN-235

**Country of Origin:** Spain and Indonesia.
**Type:** Regional airliner and general purpose transport.
**Power Plant:** Two 1,700 shp (1 268 kW) General Electric CT7-7A turboprops.
**Performance:** Max cruising speed, 244 kts (452 km/h) at 15,000 ft (4 575 m); range with max payload, 208 naut mls (385 km); range with max fuel, 2,110 naut mls (3 910 km).
**Accommodation:** Flight crew of two and up to 44 passengers four-abreast with single aisle at 30-in (76-cm) pitch; typical layout for 40 passengers.
**Status:** First of two prototypes flown in Spain on 11 November 1983 and second in Indonesia on 31 December 1983. First flight of initial production aircraft on 19 August 1986, with Spanish and Indonesian certification in June 1986 and full FAA certification on 3 December 1986. First production delivery (to Merpati Nusantara) 15 December 1986.
**Sales:** Commercial customers with confirmed orders or options by end-1986 include Merpati Nusantara, Bouraq, Dirgantara, Deraya Air Taxi, Mandala and Aviaco. The total orders by end-1986 were reported to be 115, of which 57 were for civil operators.
**Notes:** Development of the CN-235 was launched as a jointly-funded programme by CASA in Spain and IPTN in Indonesia, as a larger follow-up for the C-212 Aviocar, which is built in both countries. Production is shared, without duplication, by CASA and IPTN, with final assembly lines in each country and the programme is managed by Aircraft Technology Industries (Airtech) in Madrid.

## AIRTECH CN-235

**Dimensions:** Span, 84 ft 8 in (25,81 m); length, 70 ft 0¾ in (23,35 m); height, 26 ft 10 in (8,18 m); wing area, 645.8 sq ft (60,0 m²).
**Weights:** Operating weight empty, 20,725 lb (9 400 kg); max payload, 9,260 lb (4 200 kg); max fuel, 9,039 lb (4 100 kg); max take-off, 31,745 lb (14 400 kg); max landing, 31,305 lb (14 200 kg).

## ANTONOV AN-12

**Country of Origin:** Soviet Union.
**Type:** Medium-range freighter.
**Power Plant:** Four 4,000 ehp (2 983 kW) Ivchenko AI-20K turboprops.
**Performance:** Max cruising speed, 361 kts (670 km/h); range with max payload, 1,940 naut mls (3 600 km); range with max fuel, 3,075 naut mls (5 700 km).
**Accommodation:** Flight crew of five (two pilots, radio operator, flight engineer and navigator). Normally operates only as a freighter, with a pressurized compartment for 14 passengers; space provision for up to 100 passengers.
**Status:** An-10 first flown March 1957 and entered service with Aeroflot July 1959, followed by An-10A in February 1960. An-12 first flown 1958 (approx) and entered military service in 1959. Out of production.
**Sales:** Between 800 and 900 An-12s built (for all purposes, including military). About 200 in Aeroflot service in 1987.
**Notes:** The An-12 was evolved to meet specific Soviet needs for a military transport, based on the An-10 which was one of the first turboprop-powered airliners put into service by Aeroflot. Of generally similar appearance to the An-10 (which is now out of service), the An-12 had a redesigned fuselage with rear-loading ramp, and provision for a tail gun turret, sometimes faired over. Most of those built have gone into military service, but a sizable number is operated in 'civil' guise by Aeroflot for freight carrying and others supplied to foreign governments similarly operate in airline markings on quasi-commercial duties, carrying freight and personnel on international journeys.

## ANTONOV AN-12

**Dimensions:** Span, 124 ft 8 in (38,00 m); length, 108 ft $7\frac{1}{4}$ in (33,10 m); height, 34 ft $6\frac{1}{2}$ in (10,53 m); wing area 1,310 sq ft (121,70 m²).

**Weights** (military freighter): Empty, about 61,730 lb (28 000 kg); max payload, 44,090 lb (20 000 kg); normal take-off, 121,475 lb (55 100 kg); max take-off, 134,480 lb (61 000 kg).

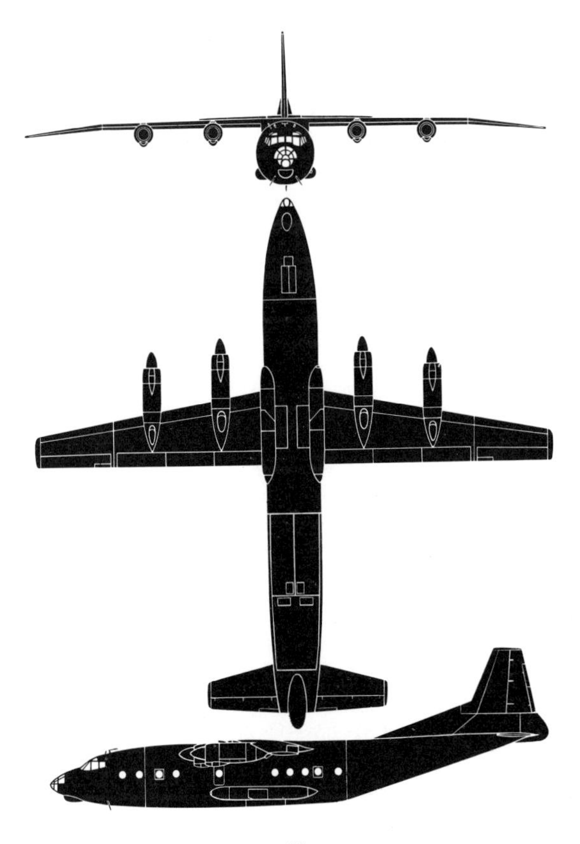

## ANTONOV AN-22

**Country of Origin:** Soviet Union.
**Type:** Long-range military and commercial freighter.
**Power Plant:** Four 15,000 shp (11 186 kW) Kuznetsov NK-12MA turboprops.
**Performance:** Max level speed, 399 kts (740 km/h); range with max payload, 2,690 naut mls (5 000 km); range with max fuel, carrying a payload of 99,200 lb (45 000 kg), 5,900 naut mls (10 950 km).
**Accommodation:** Flight crew of five or six, including two pilots, flight engineer, navigator and communications engineer. Standard layout includes a compartment for 28–29 passengers immediately behind the flight deck.
**Status:** Prototype first flown on 27 February 1965. Pre-production aircraft used on Aeroflot proving flights 1967. Production completed 1974, total built for all rôles (military and civil) believed to be less than 100.
**Sales:** No commercial sales or exports; used only by Aeroflot and Soviet military services.
**Notes:** The An-22, named Antheus, was developed to meet Soviet needs for a long-range transport with the capability of lifting outsize loads, both military and civil. Although approximately 50 An-22s are known to have operated in Aeroflot markings, these have frequently been engaged in ferrying military supplies and personnel around the world, the use of 'civil' aircraft in such cases facilitating overflights and transits through foreign countries. The extent to which the An-22 is used in a non-military rôle within the Soviet Union is not known, although its ability to carry such bulky items as earth-moving equipment and oil drilling gear is undoubtedly valuable.

## ANTONOV AN-22

**Dimensions:** Span, 211 ft 4 in (64,40 m); length, approximately 190 ft 0 in (57,92 m); height, 41 ft $1\frac{1}{2}$ in (12,53 m); wing area, 3,713 sq ft (345 m$^2$).
**Weights:** Typical empty, equipped, 251,325 lb (114 000 kg); max payload, 176,350 lb (80 000 kg); max fuel load, 94,800 lb (43 000 kg); max take-off, 551,160 lb (250 000 kg).

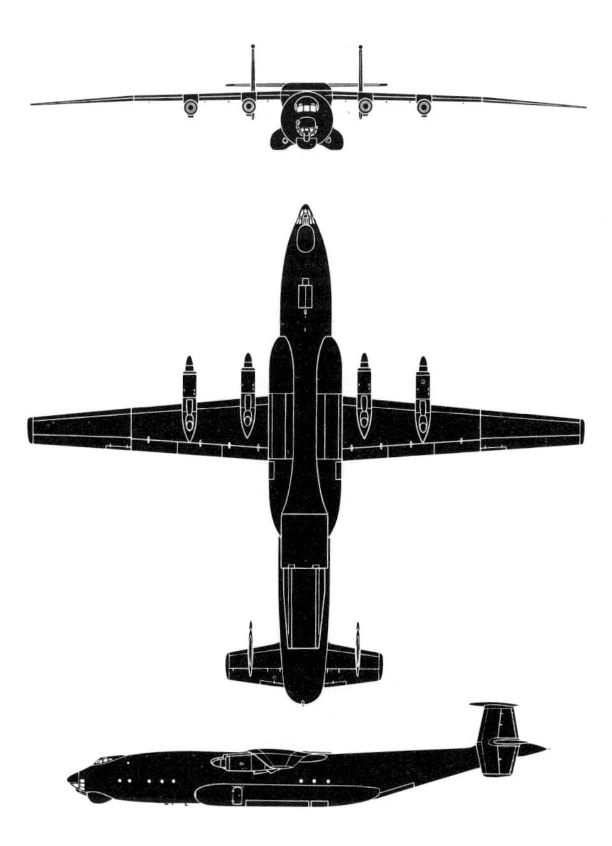

## ANTONOV AN-24 AND AN-30

**Country of Origin:** Soviet Union.
**Type:** Regional and special duty transport.
**Power Plant:** Two (An-24V) 2,530 ehp (1 887 kW) Ivchenko AI-24A or (An-26, An-30), 2,820 ehp (2 103 kW) AI-24VT turboprops.
**Performance** (An-24V): Max cruise, 269 kts (498 km/h); best-range cruise, 243 kts (450 km/h) at 19,700 ft (6 000 m); range with max payload 296 naut mls (550 km); range with max fuel, 1,293 naut mls (2 400 km).
**Accommodation:** Flight crew of up to five (two pilots, flight engineer, navigator and radio operator), but normally three for passenger-carrying flights. Up to 50 passengers, four abreast.
**Status:** An-24 prototype first flown April 1960. Service use (by Aeroflot) began in September 1963. Production completed.
**Sales:** Production total over 1,000 An-24s in all versions, primarily for Aeroflot and export to airlines of all Communist Bloc countries in East Europe and to Air Guinee, Air Mali, Cubana, CAAC in China, Egyptair, Iraqi Airways, etc.
**Notes:** The An-24 was the first Soviet transport to apply turboprop power for short-haul operations and proved among the most successful, remaining in production for some 15 years. Original basic An-24 was followed by improved An-24V; An-24T was a specialized freighter, and An-24RT and improved An-24RV had an auxiliary turbojet in the starboard nacelle to boost take-off. An-24P was developed for fire fighting and the An-30, which appeared in 1973, had a new front fuselage and was equipped for air survey and map-making. The An-26, with a rear-loading ramp, was developed and produced primarily for military use, as was the An-32 with 5,180 ehp (3 862 kW) Ivchenko AI-20M engines.

## ANTONOV AN-24V

**Dimensions:** Span, 95 ft 9½ in (29,20 m); length, 77 ft 2½ in (23,53 m); height, 27 ft 3½ in (8,32 m); wing area, 807.1 sq ft (74,98 $m^2$).
**Weights:** Empty equipped, 29,320 lb (13 300 kg); max payload, 12,125 lb (5 500 kg); max fuel, 10,494 lb (4 760 kg); max take-off and landing, 46,300 lb (21 000 kg).

## ANTONOV AN-28

**Country of Origin:** Soviet Union/Poland.
**Type:** Light general purpose transport.
**Power Plant:** Two 960 shp (716 kW) Polish-built Glushenkov TVD-10B (PZL-10S) turboprops.
**Performance:** Max cruising speed, 189 kts (350 km/h) at 9,850 ft (3 000 m); economical cruising speed, 181 kts (335 km/h); range with max payload (20 passengers), 275 naut mls (510 km); range with max fuel, 736 naut mls (1 365 km).
**Accommodation:** Flight crew of one or two; typical seating for 15 passengers three-abreast at 28-in (72-cm) pitch with offset aisle, or maximum high-density seating for 20.
**Status:** Prototype An-28 first flown in Soviet Union September 1969 (with TVD-850 engines). Pre-production An-28 first flown April 1975 after being re-engined with TVD-10Bs. First production aircraft flown in Poland, 22 July 1984; Aeroflot deliveries began 1985.
**Sales:** Soviet Union has stated a requirement for 1,200.
**Notes:** The An-28 was selected in the late 'seventies after a 'fly-off' against the Beriev Be-30, to meet Soviet requirements for a light general utility aircraft that could supplement or replace the many hundreds of An-2s and An-14s operating as transports. The prototype was at first known as the An-14M and it shares with the An-14 a high-wing layout with twin fins and rudders, but differs in having a much-enlarged fuselage and turboprop engines. The latter were at first TVD-850s but the more powerful TVD-10Bs have been adopted for the production An-28. The PZL Mielec factory in Poland has sole responsibility for producing the An-28, initially to meet Soviet requirements reported to run into many hundreds of aircraft.

# ANTONOV AN-28

**Dimensions:** Span, 72 ft 4½ in (22,07 m); length, 42 ft 11¾ in (13,10 m); height, 16 ft 1 in (4,90 m); wing area, 427.5 sq ft (39,72 $m^2$).
**Weights:** Empty equipped, 8,267 lb (3 750 kg); max payload, 4,410 lb (2 000 kg); max fuel, 3,454 lb (1 567 kg); max take-off and landing, 14,330 lb (6 500 kg).

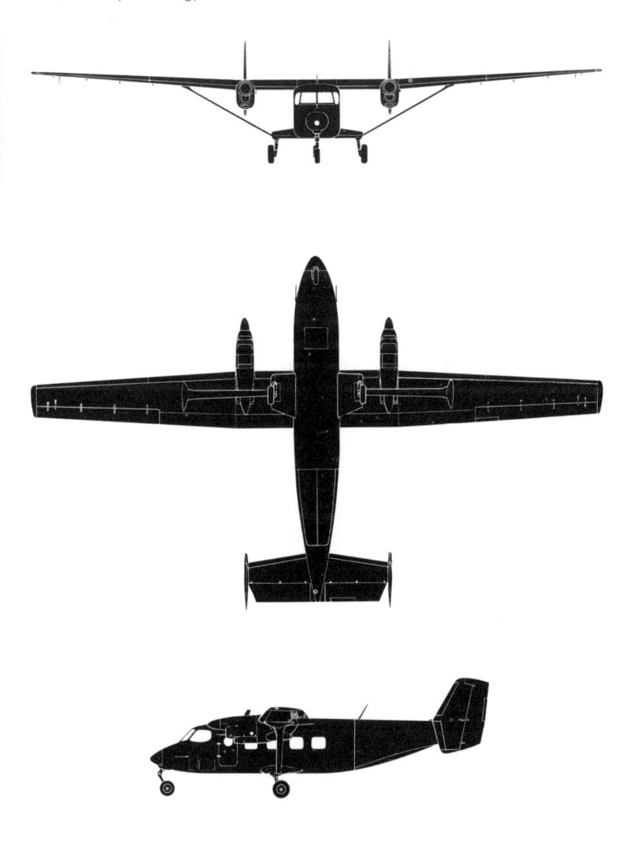

## ANTONOV AN-72 AND AN-74

**Country of Origin:** Soviet Union.
**Type:** Special purpose short-range jet transport.
**Power Plant:** Two 14,330 lb st (6 500 kgp) Lotarev D-36 turbofans.
**Performance** (An-72): Max cruising speed, 388 kts (720 km/h); range with max payload, 540 naut mls (1 000 km); range with max fuel, 2,050 naut mls (3 800 km).
**Accommodation:** Flight crew of three and up to 32 passengers on sideways-facing seats.
**Status:** Prototype flight testing of An-72 began 22 December 1977. An-74 appeared in 1984.
**Sales:** In preliminary service with Aeroflot by early 1987.
**Notes:** The An-72 is unique, as a production aircraft, in that it features upper surface blowing, a means of increasing lift by use of the Coanda effect, achieved by discharging the engine exhaust directly over the upper wing surface, and using large-area trailing-edge flaps. The system is similar to that earlier demonstrated by Boeing on its YC-14 prototypes. The An-72, with its rear loading ramp and cabin adapted for freight carrying, is intended for special duties, particularly in the more remote regions of the Soviet Union, and also has military applications. The An-74, of the same overall configuration, has many differences in detail, including wing planform, and is equipped for all-weather operations in the Polar regions, ferrying personnel and supplies. Production models of the An-72 may feature the same modifications. The An-74 is depicted in the photograph above and silhouette opposite.

## ANTONOV AN-74

**Dimensions:** Span, 84 ft 9 in (25,83 m); length, 87 ft $2\frac{1}{4}$ in (26,58 m); height, 27 ft $0\frac{1}{4}$ in (8,24 m); wing area, 969 sq ft (90 $m^2$).
**Weights:** Max payload, 22,045 lb (10 000 kg); max take-off, 72,750 lb (33 000 kg); max take-off weight (STOL operation), 58,420 lb (26 500 kg).

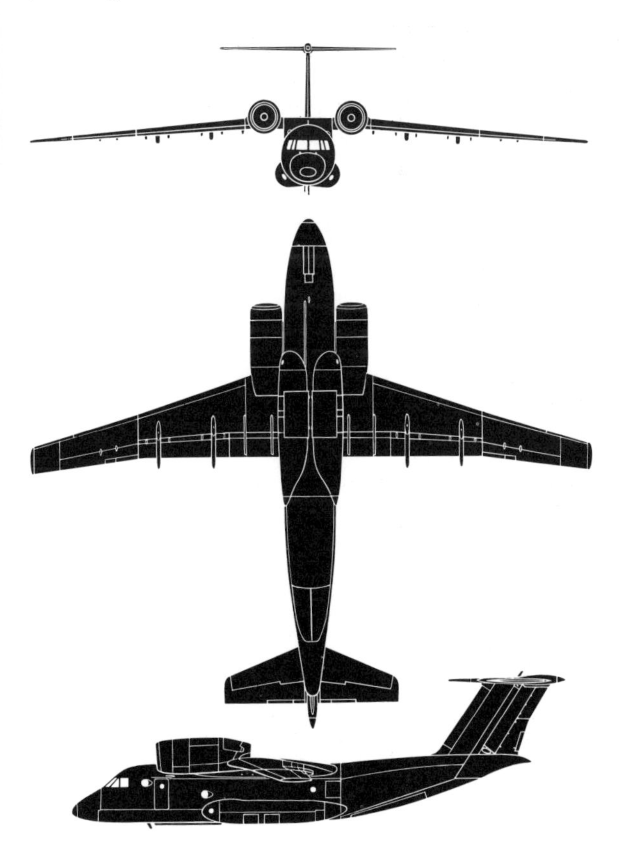

## ANTONOV AN-124

**Country of Origin:** Soviet Union.
**Type:** Long-range heavy duty transport.
**Power Plant:** Four 51,650 lb st (23 430 kgp) Lotarev D-18T turbofans.
**Performance:** Max cruising speed, 467 kts (865 km/h); long-range cruising speed, 432–459 kts (800–850 km/h) at 32,800–39,370 ft (10 000–12 000 m); range with max payload, 2,430 naut mls (4 500 km); range with max fuel, 8,900 naut mls (16 500 km).
**Accommodation:** Flight crew of four. Up to 88 passengers on upper deck aft of flight deck.
**Status:** Prototype first flight on 26 December 1982. In service, 1986.
**Sales:** Used only by Aeroflot and Soviet military forces.
**Notes:** The Antonov An-124, which made a dramatic public debut at the Paris Air Show in 1985 and was subsequently displayed in Canada and the UK in 1986, is the world's largest aircraft to date, in wing span and maximum take-off weight. Aerodynamically conventional, it makes extensive use of composites in its structure, and has a fly-by-wire control system. The 24-wheel undercarriage, including four nosewheels, allows the An-124 to operate from relatively unprepared surfaces such as hard-packed snow and ice-covered swampland. The fuselage axis can also be adjusted, up or down, to facilitate loading through the nose door or rear ramp. Primarily a military strategic freighter, the An-124 is sometimes seen operating in Aeroflot colours.

## ANTONOV AN-124

**Dimensions:** Span, 240 ft $5\frac{3}{4}$ in (73,30 m); length, 228 ft $0\frac{1}{4}$ in (69,50 m); height, 72 ft $2\frac{1}{4}$ in (22,00 m).
**Weights:** Max payload, 330,700 lb (150 000 kg); max take-off, 892,872 lb (405 000 kg).

## BEECHCRAFT C99 AIRLINER

**Country of Origin:** USA.
**Type:** Commuter airliner.
**Power Plant:** Two Pratt & Whitney PT6A-36 turboprops, flat-rated to 715 shp (533 kW) each.
**Performance:** Max cruise 245 kts (454 km/h) at 16,000 ft (4 875 m) and 249 kts (461 km/h) at 8,000 ft (2 440 m); range with max payload, 578 naut mls (1 070 km); range with max fuel, 910 naut mls (1 686 km).
**Accommodation:** Flight crew of one or two and up to 15 passengers at 28/32-in (71/81-cm) pitch, two-abreast with central aisle.
**Status:** Prototype (as a long-fuselage Queen Air) first flown December 1965, and (with PT6A-20 turboprops) in July 1966. Certification of Beech Model 99 on 2 May 1968. Improved Commuter C99 first flown 20 June 1980 with certification July 1981. First C99 customer deliveries 30 July 1981.
**Sales:** Total of 164 Beech 99 and 99A built. Total of 63 C99s sold; production ended in 1985. Early customers for the C99 include Christman Air Systems, Sunbird Airlines and Wings West.
**Notes:** The Beech 99 was evolved from the Queen Air, from which it differed primarily in having a longer fuselage and turboprop engines, and was intended primarily for third-level airline use. Production was stopped in 1975, but the basic design was upgraded in 1979, with more powerful engines and other changes, to allow Beech to re-enter the commuter airline market; sales began well but suffered in 1982/83 from the effects of the general business recession and production was brought to an end in 1985.

## BEECHCRAFT C99 AIRLINER

**Dimensions:** Span, 45 ft $10\frac{1}{2}$ in (13,98 m); length, 44 ft $6\frac{3}{4}$ in (13,58 m); height, 14 ft $4\frac{1}{2}$ in (4,38 m); wing area, 279.7 sq ft (25,99 m$^2$).
**Weights:** Operational empty, 6,494 lb (2 946 kg); max payload, 3,250 lb (1 474 kg); max fuel, 2,466 lb (1 118 kg); max take-off, 11,300 lb (5 126 kg); max landing, 11,300 lb (5 126 kg).

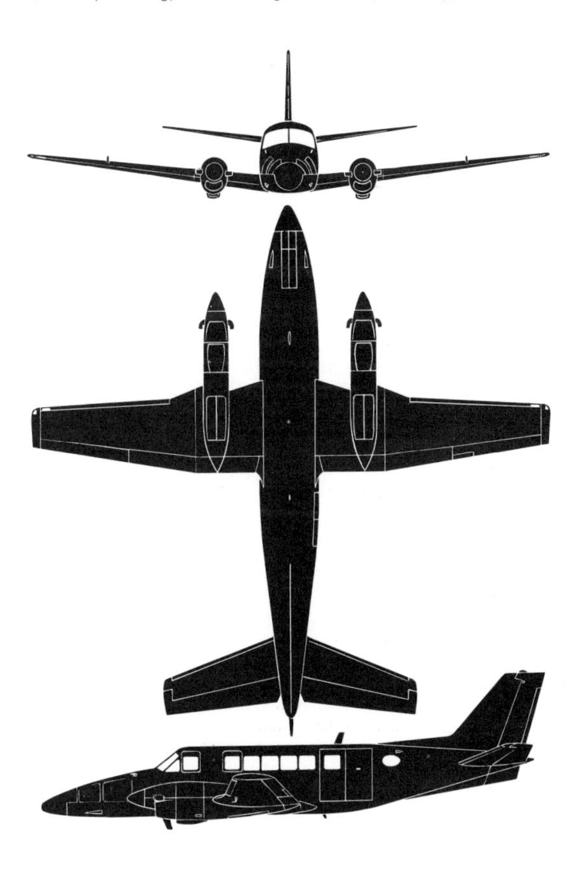

## BEECHCRAFT 1900 AIRLINER

**Country of Origin:** USA.
**Type:** Regional airliner.
**Power Plant:** Two 1,100 shp (820 kW) Pratt & Whitney PT6A-65B turboprops.
**Performance:** Max cruise, 256 kts (474 km/h) at 8,000 ft (2,440 m); long-range cruise, 217 kts (402 km/h) at 10,000 ft (3 050 m); max fuel range 794 naut mls (1 471 km) at 25,000 ft (7 620 m).
**Accommodation:** Flight crew of two and up to 19 passengers at 30-in (76-cm) pitch in individual seats with central aisle.
**Status:** First of three flying prototypes commenced flight test 3 September 1982; certification on 22 November 1983 with first deliveries immediately following.
**Sales:** Total of 60 Beech 1900s of all types sold by late 1986.
**Notes:** Beech Aircraft developed the 1900 Airliner as part of its commitment to re-enter this part of the market, after stopping production of the Beech 99 in 1975. Two versions of the Super King Air 200 were studied—the Model 1300 with the standard fuselage and the 1900 with lengthened fuselage and uprated engines; the latter only proceeded and has become available in the 1900 Airliner and, for business use, as the King Air Exec-Liner. Flight testing of the PT6A-65 engines for the Beech 1900 began on 30 April 1981 in a Super King Air test-bed, and wind tunnel testing of the aircraft configuration led to 'tail-ets' on the tailplane tips, 'stabilons' on the lower rear fuselage and vortex generators at the wing leading edge/fuselage junction. A 'wet' wing containing an additional 204 Imp gal (927 l) of fuel became available in 1986.

## BEECHCRAFT 1900 AIRLINER

**Dimensions:** Span, 54 ft 6 in (16,61 m); length, 57 ft 10 in (17,63 m); height, 14 ft 10¾ in (4,53 m); wing area, 303 sq ft (28,16 $m^2$).
**Weights:** Standard empty weight, 8,700 lb (3 947 kg); max payload, 5,300 lb (2 404 kg); max fuel weight, 2,848 lb (1 292 kg); max take-off, 16,600 lb (7 530 kg); max landing, 16,100 lb (7 302 kg); max zero fuel, 14,000 lb (6 350 kg).

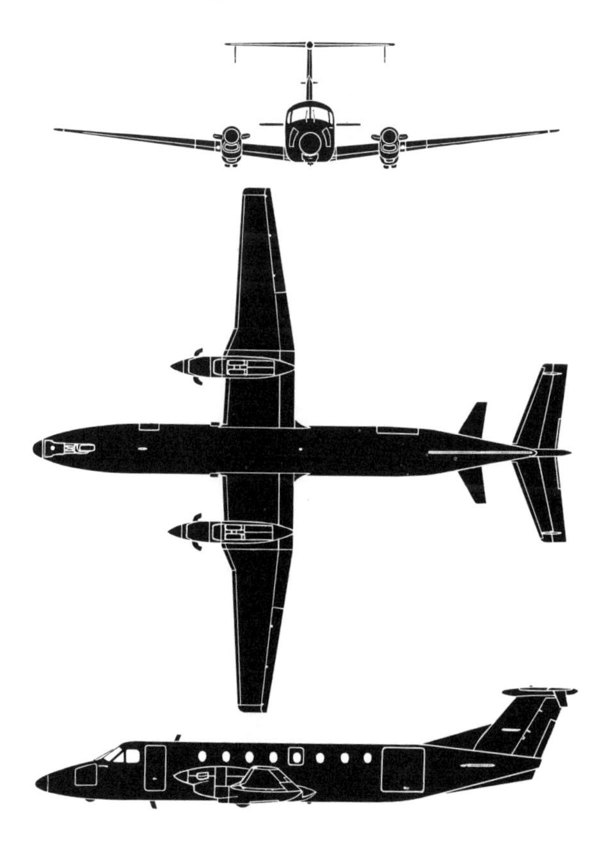

## BOEING 707-320

**Country of Origin:** USA.
**Type:** Long-range jet transport.
**Power Plant:** Four 18,000 lb st (8 165 kgp) Pratt & Whitney JT3D-3 or 19,000 lb st (8 618 kgp) JT3D-7 turbofans.
**Performance** (-320C): Max cruising speed, 525 kts (973 km/h) at 25,000 ft (7 620 m); long-range cruise, 464 kts (860 km/h) at 35,000 ft (10 670 m); range with max passenger payload, 3,735 naut mls (6 920 km); range with max fuel and 147 passengers, 5,000 naut mls (9 265 km).
**Accommodation:** Flight crew of three or four and up to 189 passengers six-abreast with central aisle at a pitch of 32-in (81-cm).
**Status:** First 707-320 flown 11 January 1959, certificated 15 July 1959, entered service (Pan American) 26 August 1959. First 707-420 flown 20 May 1959, certificated (USA) 12 February and (UK) 27 April 1960; entered service (BOAC) May 1960. First 707-320B flown 31 January 1962, certificated 31 May 1962, entered service (Pan American) June 1962. First 707-320C flown 19 February 1963, certificated 30 April 1963, entered service (Pan American) June 1963. Production complete (except military variants).
**Sales:** Overall 707/720 sales total by end-1986, 988, of which 110 military or non-commercial. Commercial 707-320 sales totalled 69 and 707-420, 37; 707-320B/-320C sales for commercial use totalled 482.
**Notes:** The Intercontinental 707-320 emerged as a longer version of the 707-120 with extra wing area, at first with turbojets but in its -320B and (with cargo door) -320C version, with turbofans. Some 250 Boeing 707s were in airline service in 1987, mostly -320Bs and -320Cs.

## BOEING 707-320B

**Dimensions:** Span, 145 ft 8½ in (44,42 m); length, 152 ft 11 in (45,60 m); height, 42 ft 5½ in (12,94 m); wing area, 3,050 sq ft (283,4 m²).

**Weights:** Operating weight empty, 146,400 lb (66 406 kg); max payload, 53,900 lb (24 450 kg); max fuel, 159,560 (72 375 kg); max zero fuel, 230,000 lb (104 330 kg); max take-off, 333,600 lb (151 315 kg); max landing, 247,000 lb (112 037 km).

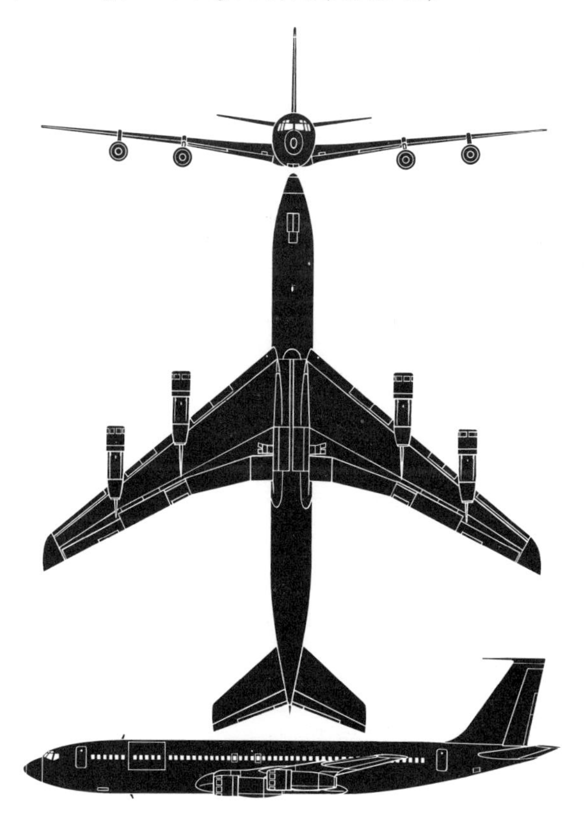

## BOEING 727

**Country of Origin:** USA.
**Type:** Short/medium-range jet transport.
**Power Plant:** Three 14,500 lb st (6 577 kgp) Pratt & Whitney JT8D-9A or 15,500 lb st (7 031 kgp) JT8D-15 or 16,000 lb st (7 258 kgp) JT8D-17 or 17,400 lb st (7 893 kgp) JT8D-17R (with automatic thrust reserve) turbofans.
**Performance:** Max cruise, 530 kts (982 km/h) at 25,000 ft (7 620 m); economical cruise, 467 kts (865 km/h); range with max payload, 2,140 naut mls (3 966 km); range with max fuel, 2,400 naut mls (9 447 km).
**Accommodation:** Flight crew of three and up to 189 passengers six-abreast with central aisle, at 30-in (76-cm) seat pitch.
**Status:** First 727-100 flown on 9 February 1963, certificated on 24 December 1963 and entered service (Eastern Airlines) on 1 February and (United) 6 February 1964. First 727C (with cargo door and handling system) flown 30 December 1964, certificated 13 January 1966, entered service (Northwest Orient) 23 April 1966. First 727-200 flown 27 July 1967, certificated 29 November 1967, entered service (Northeast Airlines) 14 December 1967. First Advanced 727 flown 3 March 1972, certificated 14 June 1972, entered service (All Nippon Airways) July 1972. First flight with automatic thrust reserve (ATR), 27 May 1976. First -200F flown 28 April 1983. Last aircraft delivered 18 September 1984.
**Sales:** Grand total of 1,831 Boeing 727s sold includes 1,249 727-200 and Advanced 727-200s.
**Notes:** The Boeing 727 tri-jet, second of the Boeing family of jetliners, remained the world's most-produced civil transport in 1986, although production has now ended.

## BOEING 727-200

**Dimensions:** Span, 108 ft 0 in (32,92 m); length, 153 ft 2 in (46,69 m); height, 34 ft 0 in (10,36 m); wing area, 1,700 sq ft (157,9 m²).
**Weights:** Operating weight empty (typical), 101,773 lb (46 164 kg); max payload, 41,000 lb (18 594 kg); standard fuel, 54,010 lb (24 498 kg); max fuel, 59,750 lb (27 102 kg); max take-off, 184,800–209,500 lb (83 820–95 027 kg); max landing, 154,500–161,000 lb (70 080–73 028 kg).

## BOEING 737-200

**Country of Origin:** USA.
**Type:** Short/medium-range jet transport.
**Power Plant:** Two 14,500 lb st (6 577 kgp) Pratt & Whitney JT8D-9A or 15,500 lb st (7 031 kgp) JT8D-15 or 16,000 lb st (7 258 kgp) JT8D-17 or 17,400 lb st (7 893 kgp) JT8D-17R (with automatic thrust reserve) turbofans.
**Performance:** Max cruising speed, 488 kts (903 km/h) at 25,000 ft (7 620 m); long-range cruise, 420 kts (778 km/h) at 35,000 ft (10 670 m); range with 115 passengers, 1,855 naut mls (3 437 km); range, high-gross weight version, 2,530 naut mls (4 688 km).
**Accommodation:** Flight crew of two or three at customer's option and up to 130 passengers six-abreast with central aisle at 30-in (76-cm) seat pitch.
**Status:** First 737-100 flown 9 April 1967 and first 737-200 (fifth 737) flown on 8 August 1967. Certification, -100 on 15 December 1967 and -200 on 21 December 1967. Entered service (-100, Lufthansa) on 10 February 1968 and (-200, United) 28 April 1968. First Advanced 737-200 flown on 15 April 1971, certificated 3 May and entered service (All Nippon Airways) June 1971.
**Sales:** Grand total of 1,746 Boeing 737s sold by late 1986, including 977 Model -200s and 104 Model 200Cs for commercial use. Production of 737-100 complete; 30 built.
**Notes:** Boeing 737 is the 'baby' of the Boeing jetliner family, launched on 19 February 1965 on the basis of an order from Lufthansa, but the 737-100 specified by the German airline was quickly superseded by the 6-ft (1,82-m) longer 737-200. The 'stretched' 737-300 and 737-400 variants are described on following pages.

## BOEING 737-200

**Dimensions:** Span, 93 ft 0 in (28,35 m); length, 100 ft 2 in (30,53 m); height, 37 ft 0 in (11,28 m); wing area, 1,098 sq ft (102,00 m²).
**Weights:** Operating weight empty, 60,210 lb (27 310 kg); max payload 34,790 lb (15 780 kg); max fuel, 39,855 lb (18,078 kg); max zero fuel, 95,000 lb (43 091 kg); max take-off, 115,500 lb–128,100 lb (52 390–58 105 kg); max landing, 103,000–107,000 lb (46 720–48 534 kg).

## BOEING 737-300

**Country of Origin:** USA.
**Type:** Short-to-medium range jet transport.
**Power Plant:** Two 20,000 lb st (9 072 kgp) CFM International CFM56-3B1 or 22,000 lb st (10 000 kgp) CFM56-3B2 turbofans.
**Performance:** Max cruising speed, 491 kts (908 km/h) at 26,000 ft (7 925 m); long-range cruising speed, 429 kts (794 km/h) at 35,000 ft (10 670 m); range with 141-passenger payload and standard fuel, 1,390 naut mls (2 570 km); range with max payload, 950 naut mls (1 760 km).
**Accommodation:** Flight crew of two and up to 141 passengers six-abreast with single aisle at 32-in (81-cm) pitch; typical mixed-class layout for eight first-class and 120 tourist.
**Status:** Development and production go-ahead for -300 on 26 March 1981. Flight test aircraft first flown on 24 February, 2 March and 4 May 1984. FAA certification 14 November 1984, first deliveries 28 November, first revenue service (Southwest Airlines), 7 December 1984. Launch of -400 on 4 June 1986, for first flight January 1988 and deliveries starting September 1988.
**Sales:** Total of 549 firm sales of -300 and 66 -400 by early 1987.
**Notes:** The 737-300 was developed to take advantage of the extra power and improved economy of the CFM56 turbofan. The 737-400 has a further 9 ft 6 in (2,9 m) fuselage 'stretch', increasing accommodation to 156 in all-coach class layout. Some structural strengthening of the outer wings will allow the 737-400 to operate at higher weights, and a tail bumper will be standard. Corporate versions are designated 77-33 and 77-34 respectively.

## BOEING 737-300

**Dimensions:** Span, 94 ft 9 in (28,88 m); length, 109 ft 7 in (33,40 m); height, 36 ft 6 in (11,13 m); wing area, 1,135 sq ft (105,4 m²).
**Weights:** Operating weight empty, 69,580 lb (31 561 kg); max payload, 35,420 lb (16 067 kg); max take-off, 124,500–135,000 lb (56 473–61 235 kg); max landing, 114,000 lb (51 710 kg); max zero fuel weight, 105,000–106,500 lb (47 628–48 308 kg).

## BOEING 747-100/-200

**Country of Origin:** USA.
**Type:** Long-range large-capacity jet transport.
**Power Plant:** Four 50,000 lb st (22 680 kgp) Pratt & Whitney JT9D-7F or 54,750 lb st (24 835 kgp) JT9D-7R4G2 or 52,500 lb st (23 814 kgp) General Electric CF6-50E2 or 53,110 lb st (24 090 kgp) Rolls-Royce 2B.211–524D4 turbofans.
**Performance:** Max cruising speed, 507 kts (939 km/h) at 35,000 ft (10 670 m); long-range cruising speed, 484 kts (896 km/h) at 35,000 ft (10 670 m); range with full passenger payload, 6,150 naut mls (11 397 km); range with max fuel, 7,100 naut mls (13 158 km).
**Accommodation:** Flight crew of three and up to 516 passengers ten-abreast with twin aisles.
**Status:** First 747 flown 9 February 1969, certificated 30 December 1969, entered service (Pan American), 21 January 1970. First -200 flown 11 October 1970, certificated 23 December 1970, entered service (KLM) early 1971. First 747F flown 30 November 1971, certificated 7 March 1972, entered service (Lufthansa) 7 March 1972. First 747C flown 23 March 1973, certificated 24 April 1973, entered service with World Airways. First 747SR flown 4 September 1973. First flight with CF6 engines 26 June 1973, first with RB.211 engines, 3 September 1976. First 747SP flown 4 July 1975, certificated 4 February 1976, entered service (Pan Am) May 1976.
**Sales:** Total of 765 commercial sales (all models) by early 1987 including 167 -100, 36 -100B/SR, 249 -200B, 76 Combi, 13 -200C, 55 -200F and 43 SP.

## BOEING 747-200

**Dimensions:** Span, 195 ft 8 in (59,64 m); length, 231 ft 10 in (70,66 m); height, 63 ft 5 in (19,33 m); wing area, 5,500 sq ft (511 m²).
**Weights:** Operating weight empty, 375,170 lb (170 180 kg); max payload, 151,500 lb (68 719 kg); max fuel, 353,760 lb (160 463 kg); max take-off, 800,000–833,000 lb (362 875–377 840 kg); max landing, 564,000–630,000 lb (255 825–285 765 kg).

## BOEING 747-300/-400

**Country of Origin:** USA.
**Type:** Very long range large capacity transport.
**Power Plant:** Four 54,750 lb st (24 834 kgp) Pratt & Whitney JT9D-7R4G2 or 52,500 lb st (23 814 kgp) General Electric CF6-50E2 or 59,000 lb st (26 762 kgp) CF6-80C2 or 53,110 lb st (24 090 kgp) Rolls-Royce RB.211-524D4 turbofans.
**Performance:** Max cruising speed, 507 kts (939 km/h) at 35,000 ft (10 670 m); long-range cruising speed, 490 kts (907 km/h) at 35,000 ft (10 670 m); range with full passenger payload, 5,650 naut mls (10 463 km).
**Accommodation:** Flight crew of three and up to 624 passengers (in high-density -300SR); typical mixed class layout for 18 first class, 52 business class and 397 economy class, respectively at 62-in (1,57-m), 36-in (91-cm) and 34-in (86-cm) pitch.
**Status:** First -300 flown 5 October 1982 with JT9D-7R4G2 engines and second flown 10 December 1982 with CF6-50E2 engines. Certificated 7 March 1983, entered service 28 March 1983 (Swissair, JT9D engines), 1 April 1983 (UTA, CF6-50 engines) and 25 November 1984 (Qantas, RB.211-524D4 engines). 747-400 launched October 1985, for service entry November 1988.
**Sales:** Total of 765 sold for commercial users (all models—see previous pages also) by early 1987, including 50 -300, 15 -300 Combi, two -300SR and 66 -400.
**Notes:** The principal new feature of the 747-300 is the extended upper deck, a 15-ft (7,11-m) lengthening of the passenger deck behind the flight deck. The -400, to enter service in 1988, introduces extended wing tips with winglets, a two-crew flight deck and structural and system changes.

## BOEING 747-300

**Dimensions:** Span, 195 ft 8 in (59,64 m); length, 231 ft 10 in (70,66 m); height, 63 ft 5 in (19,33 m); wing area 5,500 sq ft (511 m$^2$).
**Weights:** Operating weight empty, 384,480 lb (174 400 kg); max payload, 151,000 lb (68 492 kg); max fuel, 353,760 lb (160 463 kg); max take-off, 800,000–833,000 lb (362 875–377 840 kg); max landing, 574,000–630,000 lb (260 360–285 765 kg).

## BOEING 757

**Country of Origin:** USA.
**Type:** Short/medium-range jet transport.
**Power Plant:** Two 37,400 lb st (16 965 kgp) Rolls-Royce RB.211-535C or 40,100 lb st (18 190 kgp) RB.211-535E4 or 38,200 lb st (17 329 kgp) Pratt & Whitney PW 2037 turbofans.
**Performance** (RB.211 engines, basic aircraft): Max cruise, 505 kts (935 km/h) at 29,000 ft (8 839 m); long-range cruise, 459 kts (850 km/h) at 37,000 ft (11 278 m); range with max payload 3,180 naut mls (5 890 km).
**Accommodation:** Flight crew of two and up to 239 passengers six-abreast with central aisle at 32-in (81-cm) seat pitch; typical mixed class layout for 178 with four-abreast at 38-in (97-cm) pitch and six-abreast at 34-in (86-cm) pitch.
**Status:** First of five flight test and development aircraft flown on 19 February 1982 and second on 28 March 1982. Certification, (FAA) 21 December 1982, (CAA) 14 January 1983. First services (Eastern) 1 January 1983, (British Airways) 9 February 1983. First flight with PW 2037 engines 14 March 1984.
**Sales:** Total of 207 firm sales to 19 airlines by early 1987, including one -200 Combi and 20 -200 PF package freighters.
**Notes:** Boeing launched the 757 into full development and production on 23 March 1979. Earlier project activity had proceeded under the 7-N-7 generic title as Boeing searched for the correct formula for an aircraft designed to succeed the 727. The 757PF is a pure freighter, with no cabin windows, designed for the small package carriers, and the 757 Combi has the same forward port side cargo door. The designation 77-52 applies to the Corporate version that is also available to order.

## BOEING 757-200

**Dimensions:** Span, 124 ft 10 in (38,05 m); length, 155 ft 3 in (47,32 m); height, 44 ft 6 in (13,56 m); wing area, 1,994 sq ft (185,25 m²).
**Weights** (RB-211 engines): Operating weight empty, 126,250 lb (57 266 kg); max payload, 57,530 lb (26 090 kg); max zero fuel, 184,000 lb (83 460 kg); max take-off, 230,000–240,000 lb (104 325–108 860 kg); max landing, 198,000 lb (89 810 kg).

## BOEING 767-200

**Country of Origin:** USA.
**Type:** Medium-range jet transport.
**Power Plant:** Two 48,000 lb st (21 770 kgp) Pratt & Whitney JT9D-7R4D or General Electric CF6-80A turbofans.
**Performance** (JT9D engines): Max cruise speed, 484 kts (897 km/h) at 39,000 ft (11 887); long-range cruise, 459 kts (850 km/h) at 39,000 ft (11 887 m); range with max payload, 2,495 naut mls (4 620 km); range with max fuel, 6,210 naut mls (11 500 km).
**Accommodation:** Flight crew of two and up to 255 passengers seven-abreast or 290 eight-abreast with two aisles at 30-in (76-cm) seat pitch; typical mixed-class layout for 18F, six-abreast at 38-in (96.5-cm) pitch, and 202 tourist seven-abreast at 33-in (84-cm) pitch.
**Status:** First 767-200 (company-owned, JT9D engines) flown 26 September 1981; three 767-200s (United Airlines, JT9D engines) for flight/test development flown 4 November, 28 December and 30 December 1981. Certification, 30 July 1982, entered service (United Airlines) 8 September 1982. First 767-200 with CF6 engines flown 19 February 1982, certificated 4 October, delivered to Delta 25 October, entered service 15 December 1982. First 767-200ER (JT9D-7R4E engines) delivered to Ethiopian Airlines 18 May 1984.
**Sales:** Total of 181 Boeing 767-200s on order by end of 1986, including 64 -200ER.
**Notes:** Launched into production on 14 July 1978 on the basis of an order by United Airlines, the 767 resulted from several years of development under the 7X7 designation. As well as the -200 version described, the -200ER is in production with more fuel and higher weights. The 767-300 and 767-400 with longer fuselages are described separately.

## BOEING 767-200

**Dimensions:** Span, 156 ft 1 in (47,57 m); length, 159 ft 2 in (48,51 m); height, 52 ft 0 in (15,85 m); wing area, 3,050 sq ft (283,3 m²).

**Weights** (-200 basic): Operating weight empty, 180,300 lb (81 783 kg); max payload, 92,253 lb (41 845 kg); max zero fuel, 248,000 lb (112 490 kg); max take-off, 300,000 lb (136 080 kg); max landing, 270,000 lb (122 470 kg); max take-off, high gross weight options, 315,000–335,000 lb (142 884–151 956 kg).

## BOEING 767-300/-400

**Country of Origin:** USA.
**Type:** Medium-to-long range jet transport.
**Power Plant:** Two 50,000 lb st (22 680 kgp) Pratt & Whitney JT9D-7R4E or General Electric CF6-80A2 turbofans or (-300ER) 59,000 lb st (26 762 kgp) CF6-80C2 or Pratt & Whitney PW4059 turbofans.
**Performance:** Max cruising speed, 484 kts (897 km/h) at 39,000 ft (11 887 m); long-range cruising speed, 459 kts (850 km/h) at 39,000 ft (11 887 m); range with max payload 2,820 naut mls (5 220 km); range with max fuel, 5,220 naut mls (9 670 km).
**Accommodation:** Flight crew of two and up to 330 passengers eight-abreast with two aisles, typical mixed-class layout for 269.
**Status:** First order for -300 placed on 29 September 1983 by Japan Air Lines. First aircraft (with JT9D-7R4D engines) flown on 30 January 1986; second aircraft (with CF6-80A2 engines) flown in March. FAA certification on 22 September 1986 and first delivery to JAL on 25 September, for inauguration of service on 20 October.
**Sales:** Total of 214 firm sales of Boeing 767s by early 1987, includes 30 of the -300 variant.
**Notes:** Based on the airframe of the -200ER, the 737-300 has a fuselage lengthened by 21 ft 1 in (6,42 m). A long-range -300ER is also on offer, with extra fuel in the centre-section and a gross weight of 380,000 lb (172 365 kg). The 767-400 was projected during 1986, with another 21 ft 1 in (6,42 m) extension of the fuselage to increase maximum seating to 370. The weights and engines of the 767-400 will be as for the basic 767-300.

## BOEING 767-300

**Dimensions:** Span, 156 ft 1 in (47,57 m); length, 180 ft 3 in (54,94 m); height, 52 ft 0 in (15,85 m); wing area 3,050 sq ft (283,3 m²).
**Weights:** Operating weight empty, 188,800 lb (85 638 kg); max payload, 89,200 lb (40 460 kg); max fuel, 112,725 lb (51 131 kg); max take-off, 345,000–352,200 lb (156 489–159 755 kg); max landing, 300,000 lb (136 078 kg).

## BRITISH AEROSPACE ATP

**Country of Origin:** United Kingdom.
**Type:** Short-range regional airliner.
**Power Plant:** Two 2,150 shp (1 604 kW) Pratt & Whitney PW124 turboprops with 250 shp (187 kW) extra automatic emergency reserve or PW125 with 350 shp (261 kW) reserve.
**Performance:** Cruising speed, 265 kts (491 km/h); range with max payload, 575 naut mls (1 065 km); range with max fuel, 1,860 naut mls (3 444 km).
**Accommodation:** Flight crew of two and up to 72 passengers; typical layout for 64, four-abreast with single aisle of 31-in (79-cm) seat pitch.
**Status:** Marketing launch in September 1982 followed by full-scale development launch on 1 March 1984. First flight of initial test aircraft on 6 August 1986. Certification expected 30 July 1987, with entry into service (BMA) on 28 September 1987. First deliveries to LIAT in 1988.
**Sales:** Total of five firm sales and two options by early 1987, for British Midland and Leeward Island Air Transport.
**Notes:** The ATP (Advanced Turboprop) airliner is a product of the Manchester facilities of British Aerospace, being a derivative of the HS.748. It has the same fuselage cross-section but is about 18 ft (5,49 m) longer to accommodate four more seat rows. The wing structure is basically the same, with revised wingtips, and the vertical tail has slight sweepback. New engines have six-bladed propellers and an advanced technology flight deck is incorporated designed to increase pilot efficiency and reduce workload through the use of push-button selector indication for system status, with colour-coding, miniaturised engine instruments and automatic display of malfunctions.

## BRITISH AEROSPACE ATP

**Dimensions:** Span, 100 ft 6 in (30,63 m); length, 85 ft 4 in (26,01 m); height, 23 ft 5 in (7,14 m); wing area, 843 sq ft (78,30 m$^2$).
**Weights:** Operating weight empty, 29,970 lb (13 594 kg); max payload, 14,830 lb (6 727 kg); max fuel, 11,200 lb (5 080 kg); max take-off, 49,500 lb (22 453 kg); max landing, 48,000 lb (21 773 kg).

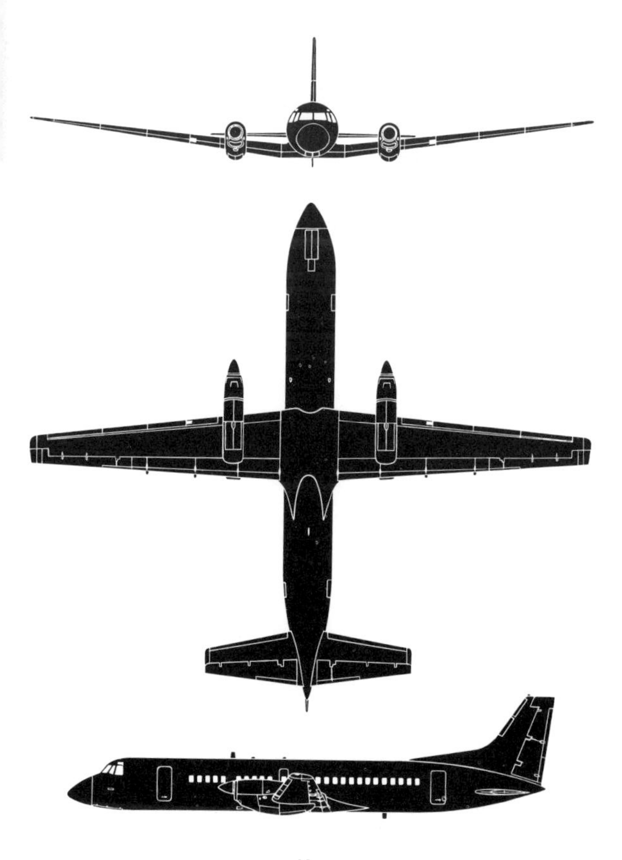

## BRITISH AEROSPACE BAe 146

**Country of Origin:** United Kingdom.
**Type:** Short-range regional transport.
**Power Plant:** Four 6,700 lb st (3 040 kgp) Avco Lycoming ALF 502R-3 or (-200) 6,970 lb st (3 162 kgp) ALF 502R-5 turbofans.
**Performance** (BAe 146-200): Max cruising speed, 423 kts (784 km/h) at 26,000 ft (7 925 m); long-range cruise, 381 kts (706 km/h) at 30,000 ft (9 145 m); range with max payload (typical reserves), 1,176 naut mls (2 179 km); range with max fuel (including options), 1,476 naut mls (2 733 km).
**Accommodation:** Flight crew of two: typical one-class seating (Srs 200) for 96; max high density arrangement, 109 passengers six-abreast at 29-in (74-cm) seat pitch.
**Status:** BAe 146-100 development aircraft flown 3 September 1981, 25 January 1982 and 2 April 1982; first BAe 146-200 flown 1 August 1982. Certification of -100 7 February 1983, first delivery (to Dan-Air) 23 May 1983. Srs 200 certificated June 1983, first delivery to Air Wisconsin 17 June and first service flown 27 June.
**Sales:** Total sales 86 by end-1986, including 20 Srs 100 and 66 Srs 200; two Srs 100 for British Royal Flight.
**Notes:** The BAe 146 was designed (as the HS.146) at Hatfield by Hawker Siddeley Aviation prior to latter's nationalization as part of British Aerospace, which launched production of the 146 in July 1978. Production is spread throughout BAe factories in the UK with final assembly at Hatfield; Avco Corp in USA and Saab-Scania in Sweden are producing wings and tail units respectively. Initial BAe 146-100 seats up to 93 and is some 8 ft (2,4 m) shorter; it is followed by the -200 which differs only in fuselage length and operating weights, and is likely to become the most numerous variant in service.

## BAe 146-200

**Dimensions:** Span, 86 ft 5 in (26,34 m); length, 93 ft 10 in (28,60 m); height, 28 ft 3 in (8,61 m); wing area, 832 sq ft (77,30 m²).
**Weights:** Typical operating weight empty, 50,500 lb (22 861 kg); max payload, 23,100 lb (10 478 kg); max usable fuel, 22,704 lb (10 298 kg); max take-off, 93,000 lb (42 184 kg); max landing, 81,000 lb (36 741 kg).

## BRITISH AEROSPACE BAE 146-300

**Country of Origin:** United Kingdom.
**Type:** Short-to-medium range jet airliner.
**Power Plant:** Four 6,970 lb st (3 162 kgp) Avco Lycoming ALF 502R-5 turbofans.
**Performance:** Best economy cruising speed, 383 kts (709 km/h) at 30,000 ft (9 150 m); ferry range with 100 passengers, 1,090 naut mls (2 202 km); ferry range with max standard fuel, 1,520 naut mls (2 817 km).
**Accommodation:** Flight crew of two and up to 112 passengers five-abreast with single aisle; typical layout for 100 five-abreast at 31-in (79-cm) seat pitch.
**Status:** Project studies revealed September 1984, construction of a prototype launched during 1986 for first flight scheduled to be made on 1 May 1987.
**Sales:** No firm sales announced. United Express (originally Air Wisconsin) holds options on the -300.
**Notes:** The -300 is the second 'stretch' of the basic 146 Srs 100. Several options were considered during the project stage and, as finally defined, a 'simple' stretch of the -200 was chosen, without the wing endplates and uprated engines at first considered. The stretch of 7 ft 10 in (2,37 m) is exactly the same extension that distinguishes the -200 from the -100, and the extra length allows the -300 to carry the same 100-passenger load as the -200, but in more comfortable five-abreast rather than six-abreast layout. Further developments of the BAe 146-300 under consideration in 1986 included weight growth to 104,000 lb (47 175 kg).

## BRITISH AEROSPACE BAE 146-300

**Dimensions:** Span, 86 ft 5 in (26,34 m); length, 101 ft 8 in (30,99 m); height, 28 ft 2 in (8,60 m); wing area, 832 sq ft (77,3 $m^2$).
**Weights:** Operating weight empty, 54,000 lb (24 494 kg); max payload, 21,500 lb (9 752 kg); max take-off, 93,000 lb (42 184 kg); max landing, 83,000 lb (37 649 kg).

## BRITISH AEROSPACE HS.748

**Country of Origin:** United Kingdom.
**Type:** Regional airliner.
**Power Plant** (Srs 2B): Two 2,280 ehp (1 982 kW) Rolls-Royce Dart RDa 7 Mk 552 turboprops.
**Performance** (Srs 2B): Typical cruising speed, 245 kts (454 km/h); max payload range, 1,007 naut mls (1 865 km) at cost economical cruise; max fuel range, 1,650 naut mls (3 055 km).
**Accommodation:** Normal flight crew of two and 48–52 passengers at 30-in (76-cm) pitch, four-abreast with central aisle.
**Status:** Two Avro 748 prototypes flown 24 June 1960 and 10 April 1961. First production Srs 1 flown 30 August 1961, certificated 7 December 1961, entered service with Skyways. Prototype Srs 2 flown 6 November 1961; certificated October 1962, entered service with BKS Air Transport. Prototype Srs 2C flown 31 December 1971. First production Srs 2B flown 22 June 1977. Super 748 first flown 30 July 1984.
**Sales:** Total of 18 Srs 1s built. Overall 748 sales total (military and civil), 380 by late 1986, including 89 assembled by HAL in India.
**Notes:** The 748 has provided steady business for what was the Avro company, now Manchester facilities of British Aerospace, since it entered production early in 1962. The Srs 1 had less powerful Dart engines and lower weights; Srs 2 and 2A differ in engine variants, Srs 2C has a large cargo loading door and Srs 2B has increased wing span and numerous product improvements. Introduced in 1983, the 748-2B Super has an advanced flight deck and engine hush-kits.

## BRITISH AEROSPACE HS.748 SERIES 2B

**Dimensions:** Span, 102 ft 6 in (31,23 m); length, 67 ft 0 in (20,42 m); height, 24 ft 10 in (7,57 m); wing area, 828.87 sq ft (77,00 m²).
**Weights:** Typical operational empty, 26,814 lb (12 163 kg); max payload, 11,686 lb (5 300 kg); max fuel, 11,520 lb (5 225 kg); max zero fuel, 38,500 lb (17 464 kg); max take-off, 46,500 lb (21 092 kg); max landing, 43,000 lb (19 505 kg).

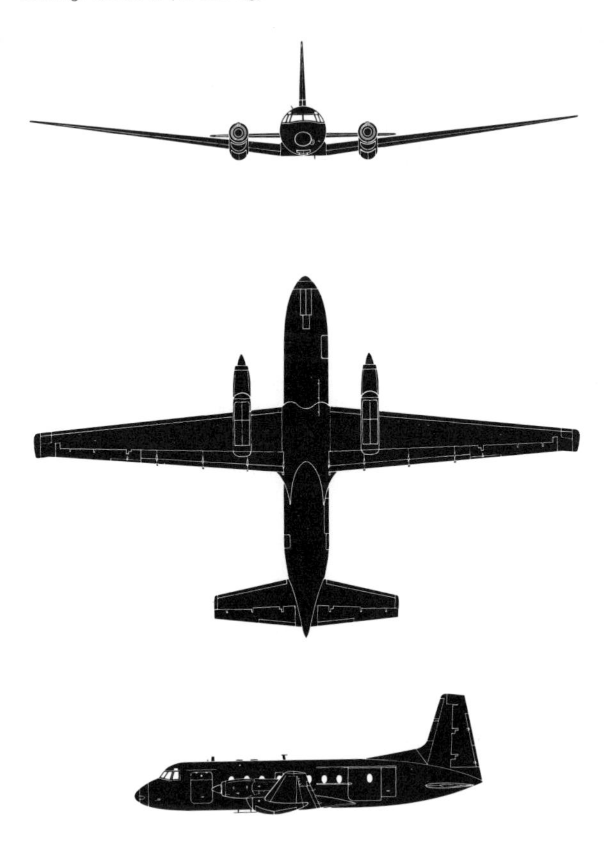

## BRITISH AEROSPACE JETSTREAM 31

**Country of Origin:** United Kingdom.
**Type:** Commuter liner and business twin.
**Power Plant:** Two 940 shp (701 kW) Garrett TPE331-10UF turboprops.
**Performance:** Max cruising speed, 263 kts (488 km/h) at 15,000 ft (4 570 m); best economy cruising speed, 230 kts (426 km/h) at 25,000 ft (7 620 m); range with 18 passengers, 675 naut mls (1 250 km); range with nine passengers, 1,065 naut mls (1 975 km).
**Accommodation:** Flight crew of two and up to 19 passengers three-abreast with off-set aisles at 30/31-in (76/79-cm) pitch.
**Status:** Prototype (derived from original Handley Page production variant) first flown on 28 March 1980. First two production Jetstream 31s flown on 18 March and 26 May 1982 respectively. British certification, 29 June 1982. Production deliveries commenced 15 December 1982 (to Contactair) and on 30th December (Peregrine).
**Sales:** Total of 148 sold by the end of 1986 plus another 32 on option and including more than 100 for seven US commuter airlines.
**Notes:** Jetstream 31 is the re-launched BAe production version of original HP.137 offered in 18/19-seat commuter, 12-seat executive shuttle and nine-seat corporate versions. The commuter version has proved to be the best seller to date, and has sold particularly well in the US where it is used by several airlines flying services in and out of the major hubs. In 1987, British Aerospace was considering launching the stretched Jetstream 41 with about 26 seats and uprated engines. Several examples of the earlier HP.137, some with US turboprops replacing the original Astazous, are still in airline use.

## BRITISH AEROSPACE JETSTREAM 31

**Dimensions:** Span, 52 ft 0 in (15,85 m); length, 47 ft $1\frac{1}{2}$ in (14,37 m); height, 17 ft 6 in (5,37 m); wing area, 271.3 sq ft (25,20 $m^2$).
**Weights:** Operational weight empty, 9,570 lb (4 341 kg); max payload, 3,980 lb (1 805 kg); max fuel weight, 3,024 lb (1 372 kg); max take-off, 15,212 lb (6 900 kg); max landing weight, 14,550 lb (6 600 kg).

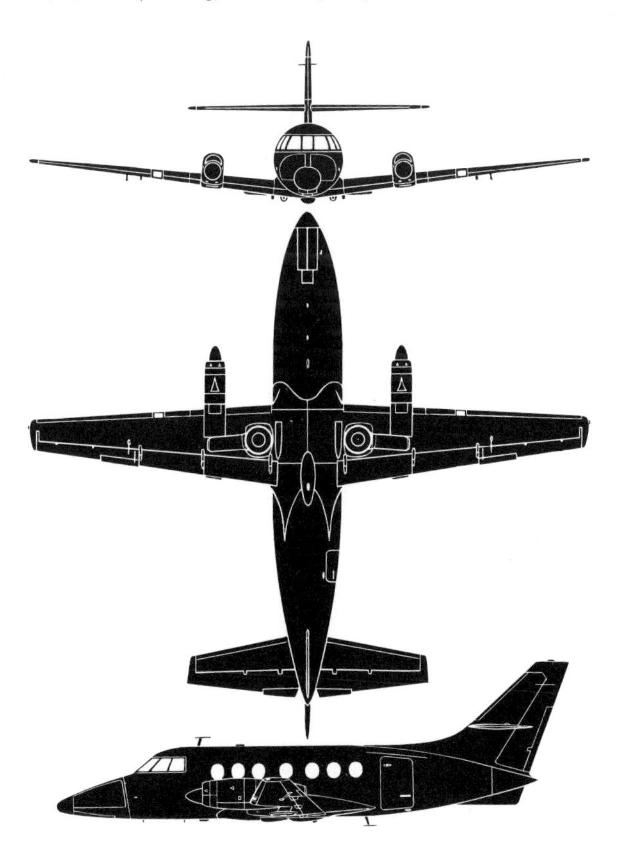

## BRITISH AEROSPACE (BAC) ONE-ELEVEN

**Country of Origin:** United Kingdom.
**Type:** Short-range jet transport.
**Power Plant** (Srs 500): Two 12,550 lb st (5 692 kgp) Rolls-Royce Spey 512 DW turbofans.
**Performance:** (Srs 500): Max cruise, 470 kts (870 km/h) at 21,000 ft (6 400 km); best economy cruise, 400 kts (742 km/h) at 25,000 ft (7 620 m); range with typical max payload, 1,480 naut mls (2 744 km); max range, 1,880 naut mls (3,484 km).
**Accommodation:** Flight crew of two and up to 119 passengers five-abreast, with off-set aisle, at 29-in (74-cm) pitch.
**Status:** Prototype first flown 20 August 1963; first production Srs 200 flown 19 December 1963, certification 6 April 1965 followed by first services on 9 April (BUA) and 25 April (Braniff). Prototype Srs 300/400 flown 13 July 1965; Srs 400 certification 22 November 1965. Prototype Srs 500 flown 30 June 1967 and first production Srs 500 on 7 February 1968 and certificated 18 August 1968. Prototype Srs 475 flown 27 August 1970 and first production on 5 April 1971, with certification in July. Production in UK complete. First Srs 560 flown in Romania 18 September 1982.
**Sales:** Total of 230 built in UK including 56 Srs 200, nine Srs 300, 69 Srs 400, nine Srs 475 and 87 Srs 500.
**Notes:** One-Eleven Srs 200, 300 and 400 are dimensionally similar; Srs 500 has longer fuselage and extended wing tips and Srs 475 has original fuselage with extended wing and uprated engines. Following delivery of last One-Eleven in mid-1982, British Aerospace supplied components for 22 more to be assembled in Romania.

## BRITISH AEROSPACE (BAC) ONE-ELEVEN SRS 500

**Dimensions:** Span, 93 ft 6 in (28,50 m); length, 107 ft 0 in (32,61 m); height, 24 ft 6 in (7,47 m); wing area, 1,031 sq ft (95,78 m$^2$).
**Weights:** Typical operating empty, 54,582 lb (24 758 kg); max payload, 26,418 lb (11 983 kg); max zero fuel, 81,000 lb (36 741 kg); max take-off, 104,500 lb (47 400 kg); max landing, 87,000 lb (39 463 kg).

## CANADAIR CL-44

**Country of Origin:** Canada.

**Type:** Long-range cargo and passenger transport.

**Power Plant:** Four 5,730 shp (4 276 kW) Rolls-Royce Tyne 515/10 turboprops.

**Performance:** Max cruising speed, 349 kts (647 km/h) at 20,000 ft (6 100 m); range with max payload, 2,850 naut mls (5 300 km); range with max fuel and 35,564-lb (16 132-kg) payload, 4,850 naut mls (8 990 km).

**Accommodation:** Flight crew of three and up to 189 passengers six-abreast with central aisle at 32-in (81-cm) pitch.

**Status:** First CL-44D (military CC-106) flown 15 November 1959; first CL-44D-4 (commercial prototype) flown 16 November 1960; first delivery (Flying Tiger) 31 May 1961. CL-44J prototype flown 8 November 1965, CL-44-O conversion flown 26 November 1969. Production completed.

**Sales:** Total of 27 CL-44D-4s built for Flying Tiger, Seaboard World, Slick and Loftleider.

**Notes:** Original CL-44D was a Canadian development from the Bristol Britannia design, with lengthened fuselage, greater wing span and new engines. Twelve were built for the RCAF as CC-106 Yukons, several passing into commercial service as freighters when retired in 1973. The CL-44D-4 was built primarily as a commercial freighter, featuring a swing-tail for straight-in loading. Loftleider used CL-44s as high density transports, including four CL-44J conversions with stretched fuselage for 214 passengers. The sole CL-44-O has an enlarged diameter upper deck. About a dozen CL-44Ds and Yukons were still in airline service, as freighters, in 1987, principally with airlines in South America and Africa.

## CANADAIR CL-44D-4

**Dimensions:** Span, 142 ft 3½ in (43,37 m); length, 136 ft 10¾ in (41,73 m); height, 38 ft 8 in (11,80 m); wing area, 2,075 sq ft (192,72 m$^2$).

**Weights:** Operating weight empty, 88,952 lb (40 345 kg); max payload, 66,048 lb (29 959 kg); max fuel, 81,448 lb (36 944 kg); max zero fuel, 155,000 lb (70 308 kg); max take-off, 210,000 lb (95 250 kg); max landing, 165,000 lb (74 843 kg).

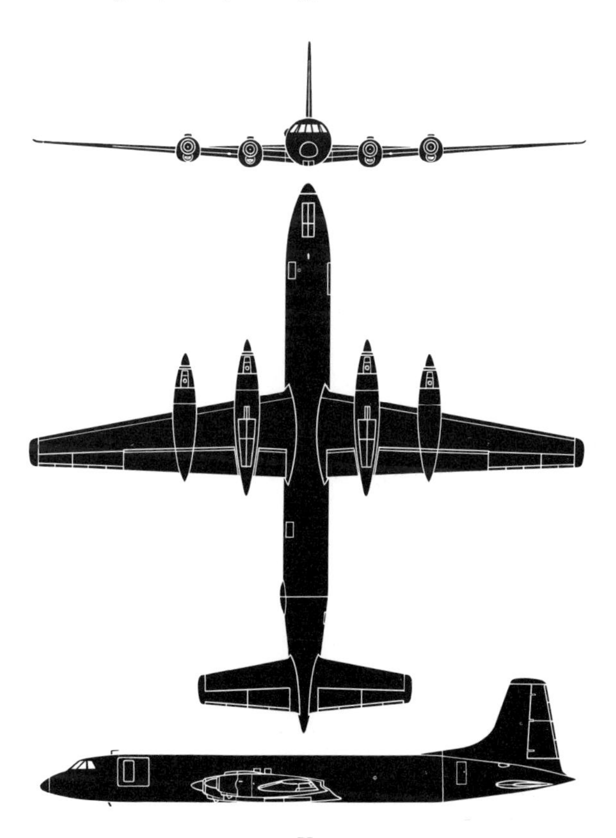

## CASA C-212 AVIOCAR

**Country of Origin:** Spain.
**Type:** Commuter airliner and general purpose light transport.
**Power Plant:** Two 900 shp (671 kW) Garrett TPE 331-10-511C turboprops.
**Performance:** Max cruise, 197 kts (365 km/h) at 10,000 ft (3 050 m); long range cruise, 187 kts (346 km/h) at 10,000 ft (3 050 m); max payload range (26 passengers), 220 naut mls (408 km/h); range with max fuel, 950 naut mls (1 760 km).
**Accommodation:** Flight crew of two and 22 passengers at 28.5-in (72-cm) pitch three-abreast with offset aisle or 28 passengers at 28.5-in (72-cm) pitch four-abreast with central aisle.
**Status:** Prototype C-212 flown 26 March 1971; 138th and 139th production aircraft became prototypes for the Srs 200, the first of these flying on 30 April 1978. Deliveries of Srs 200 commenced early 1980. Srs 300 first flown 1984, for service introduction 1987.
**Sales:** Approximately 400 sold by end 1986, for military and civil use.
**Notes:** Possessing STOL characteristics, the C-212 is available in several civil and military versions. The original Srs 100 had lower-rated TPE 331-5 engines and a gross weight of 12,500 lb (5 675 kg) or, eventually, 14,330 lb (6 500 kg). In Indonesia, IPTN assembled 29 Srs 100 aircraft before part-manufacture (up to 85 per cent of the total airframe) and final assembly switched to the NC-212 Srs 200. Launched in 1984, the Srs 300 introduces a slightly longer wing with upturned tips, a restyled and lengthened nose and Garrett TPE331-10R-513C engines. An aerodynamic fairing is an option, to replace the rear freight doors and is shown in the silhouette opposite. The photograph above illustrates the standard C-212 Srs 200.

## CASA C-212 SERIES 300 AVIOCAR

**Dimensions:** Span 62 ft 4 in (19,00 m); length, 49 ft 9 in (15,16 m); height, 20 ft 8 in (6,30 m); wing area, 430.56 sq ft (40,00 m$^2$).
**Weights:** Operational empty, 10,053 lb (4 560 kg); max payload, 6,107 lb (2 770 kg); max fuel load, 3,527 lb (1 600 kg); max zero fuel, 15,542 lb (7 050 kg); max take-off, 16,424 lb (7 450 kg); max landing, 16,203 lb (7 350 kg).

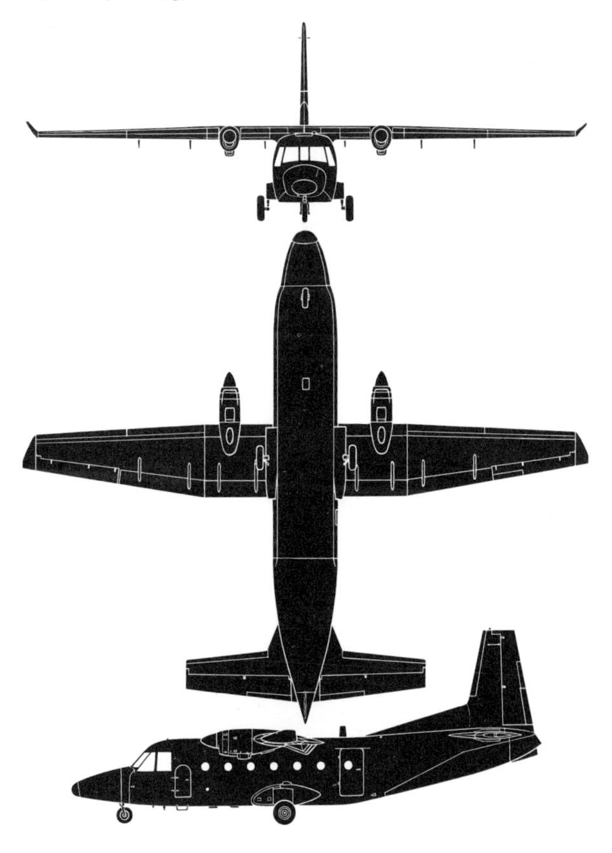

## CESSNA CARAVAN I

**Country of Origin:** USA.
**Type:** Light utility and special purpose transport.
**Power Plant:** One 600 shp (447 kW) Pratt & Whitney PT6A-114 turboprop.
**Performance:** Max cruising speed, 184 kts (341 km/h) at 10,000 ft (3 050 m); range with max fuel, 1,370 naut mls (2 539 km) at 20,000 ft (6 100 m).
**Accommodation:** Flight crew of one and up to nine passengers, two or three-abreast.
**Status:** The Cessna Model 208 was launched in 1981, and the prototype first flew on 9 December 1982. First production aircraft rolled out August 1984. FAA Type Approval 23 October 1984. Deliveries of windowless Model 208A began early in 1985. Model 208B first flew on 3 March 1986, was certificated on 9 October and first delivered on 31 October 1986.
**Sales:** Total of about 200 firm sales by early 1987, including at least 70 Model 208B.
**Notes:** The Caravan was designed by Cessna to provide a light, general utility aircraft, primarily for commercial use carrying assorted loads, but also readily adaptable to a variety of other rôles such as casualty evacuation, para-dropping of supplies or personnel, fire-fighting, aero-surveying, agricultural spraying and so on. A significant market for the type emerged when Federal Express, a specialist company in the overnight delivery of small packages, placed large orders for the Model 208A and Model 208B which have no windows, underfuselage cargo pannier and a taller fin. The Model 208B, development of which was backed by Federal Express, features a fuselage lengthened by 4 ft 0 in (1,22 m).

## CESSNA CARAVAN I

**Dimensions:** Span, 52 ft 1 in (15,88 m); length, 37 ft 7 in (11,46 m); height, 14 ft 2 in (4,32 m); wing area, 279.4 sq ft (25,96 $m^2$).
**Weights:** Operating weight empty, 3,800 lb (1 724 kg); max payload, 3,000 lb (1 361 kg); max fuel, 2,224 lb (1 009 kg); max take-off, 7,300 lb (3 311 kg); max landing, 7,300 lb (3 311 kg).

## CESSNA TWINS (AND CARAVAN II)

**Country of Origin:** USA.
**Type:** Light general purpose piston-engined transports.
**Power Plant** (Caravan II): Two 500 shp (373 kW) Pratt & Whitney Canada PT6A-112 turboprops.
**Performance** (Caravan II): Max cruising speed, 240 kts (444 km/h); best economy cruising speed, 200 kts (370 km/h); range with max fuel, 1,030 naut mls (1 908 km).
**Accommodation:** Flight crew of two and up to nine passengers two-abreast with centre aisle.
**Status:** Prototype Reims-Cessna F 406 Caravan II first flown 22 September 1983. Certification on 21 December 1984. First production Caravan II flown 20 April 1985.
**Sales:** Total of about 20 firm sales by early 1987. Many hundreds of other Cessna twin-engined types sold for air taxi and third-level airline use.
**Notes:** The Caravan II is the latest Cessna twin to reach production for the small airline/air taxi operator and business user. It is assembled exclusively by Cessna's European associate Reims Aviation, using airframe components supplied from the US. These include wings that are identical with those of the Conquest II and fuselage structures based on those of the Titan. The landing gear is also derived from the Conquest II and the engine nacelles from the Conquest I. Other Cessna twins of particular utility in the airline business include the Model 404 Titan and Model 421, both of which have 375 hp (280 kW) Continental GTSIO-520-M flat-six piston engines.

## CESSNA CARAVAN II

**Dimensions:** Span, 49 ft 5¾ in (15,08 m); length, 39 ft 0 in (11,89 m); height, 13 ft 2 in (4,01 m); wing area, 253 sq ft (23,50 m²).
**Weights:** Operating weight empty, 5,055 lb (2 293 kg); max payload, 3,446 lb (1 563 kg); max fuel, 3,183 lb (1 444 kg); max take-off, 9,360 lb (4 246 kg); max landing, 9,360 lb (4 246 kg).

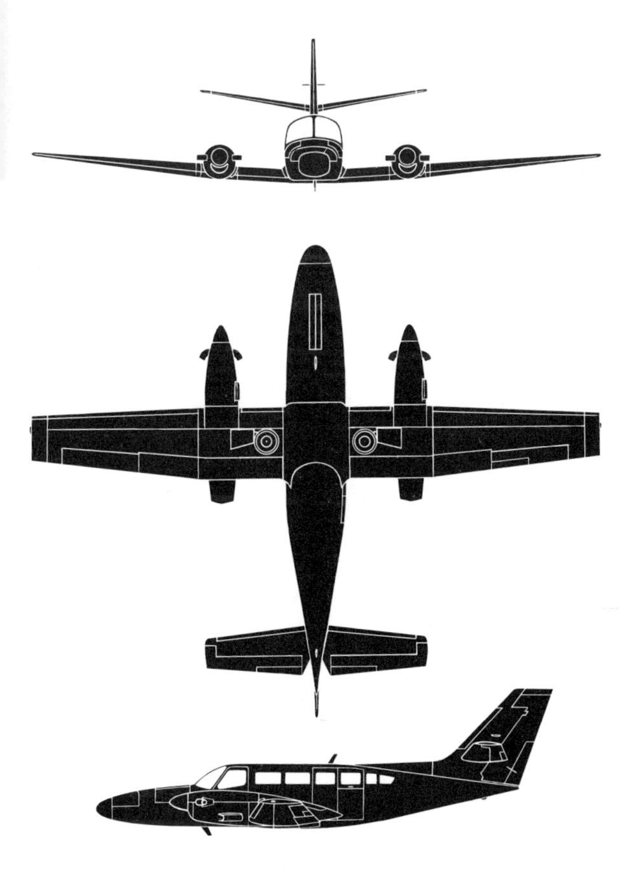

## CONVAIR 580 (AND 600, 640)

**Country of Origin:** USA. **Type:** Short-range turboprop airliner.
**Power Plant:** Two, 3,750 shp (2 800 kW) Allison 501-D13H turboprops.
**Performance:** Max cruise, 297 kts (550 km/h) at 20,000 ft (6 100 m), range with 5,000-lb (2 270-kg) payload, 1,970 naut mls (3 650 km); range with max fuel, 2,577 naut mls (4 773 km).
**Accommodation:** Flight crew of two or three, and up to 56 passengers four-abreast with central aisle, at 30-in (76-cm) pitch.
**Status:** CV-240 Turboliner prototype flown 29 December 1950 and YC-131C conversion with Allison 501D turboprops flown 29 June 1954; first CV-580 Allison-Convair flown 19 January 1960, certificated 21 April 1960 and entered airline service (Frontier) June 1964. Eland-Convair conversion flown 9 February 1955, entered airline service (Allegheny) July 1959. CV-600 (Dart engines) first flown 20 May 1965, certificated 18 November, entered service (Central Airlines) 30 November 1965; CV-640 first flown 20 August 1965, certificated 7 December 1965, entered service (Caribair) 22 December 1965. Super 580 prototype flown 21 March 1984.
**Sales:** Total of 170 CV-340s/440s converted to CV-580 of which 110 for airline use. Total of 38 CV-240s converted to CV-600 and 27 CV-340s/440s to CV-640s, for airline use. About 90 CV-580s in airline service in 1987.
**Notes:** Several schemes for converting piston-engined airliners to have turboprop engines were projected during the 'fifties, but only the Convair 240/340/440 family was adopted for such conversion on a large scale. In 1984, Allison sponsored development of the Super 580 with uprated 501-D22G engines and projected a stretched-fuselage derivative as the Allison Flagship.

## CONVAIR 580

**Dimensions:** Span, 105 ft 4 in (32,12 m); length, 81 ft 6 in (24,84 m); height, 29 ft 2 in (8,89 m); wing area, 920 sq ft (85,5 m$^2$).
**Weights:** Operating weight empty, 30,275 lb (13 732 kg); max payload, 8,870 lb (4 023 kg); max fuel, 13,887 lb (6 299 kg); max take-off, 58,140 lb (26 371 kg); max landing, 52,000 lb (23 187 kg).

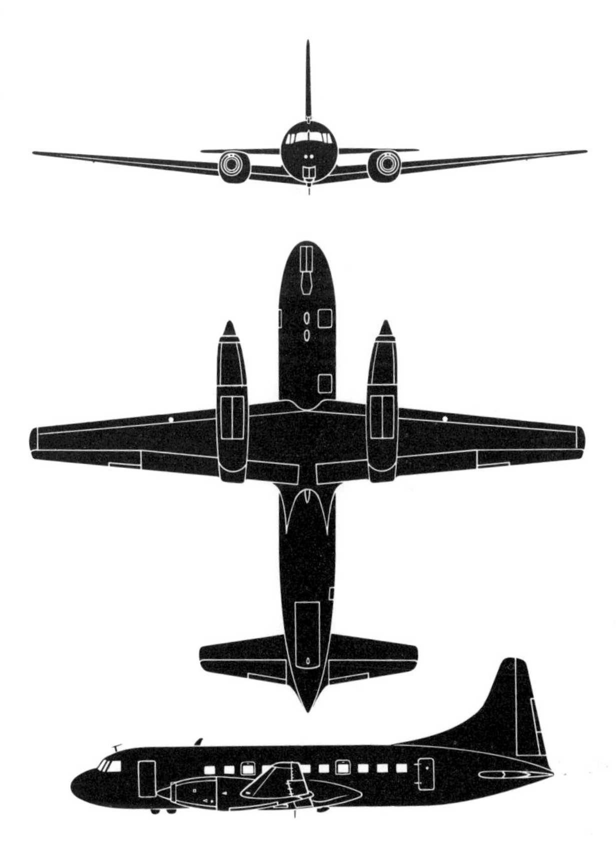

## DASSAULT-BREGUET MERCURE

**Country of Origin:** France.
**Type:** Short-range jet transport.
**Power Plant:** Two 15,500 lb st (7 030 kgp) Pratt & Whitney JT8D-15 turbofans.
**Performance:** Max cruise, 500 kts (926 km/h) at 20,000 ft (6 100 m); best economy cruise, 463 kts (858 km/h) at 30,000 ft (9 145 m); range with max payload, 600 naut mls (1 110 km); range with max fuel, 1,750 naut mls (3 240 km).
**Accommodation:** Flight crew of two; typical mixed-class seating 12F four-abreast at 38-in (96,5-cm) pitch and 108 Y six-abreast at 32-in (81,5-cm) pitch; maximum passenger capacity 162 at 30-in (76-cm) pitch.
**Status:** Two prototypes flown 28 May 1971 and 7 September 1972. First production aircraft flown 17 July 1973, certificated 12 February 1974, entered service (Air Inter) 4 June 1974. Certificated for Cat III operation 30 September 1974. Production completed.
**Sales:** Ten aircraft ordered by Air Inter 29 January 1972, all still in service together with updated second prototype; no other sales were made.
**Notes:** The Mercure was intended by Dassault to provide a basis for the company to expand its commercial activities and was put into production with only one airline order, placed by the French domestic operator Air Inter. Consequently, considerable losses were made on the programme by Dassault and the French government, as well as risk-sharing partners in Italy, Spain, Belgium, Switzerland and Canada. An attempt to launch a developed Mercure 200 with McDonnell Douglas participation did not succeed.

## DASSAULT-BREGUET MERCURE

**Dimensions:** Span, 100 ft 3 in (30,55 m); length, 114 ft $3\frac{1}{2}$ in (34,84 m); height 37 ft $3\frac{1}{4}$ in (11,36 m); wing area, 1,249 sq ft (116,0 m²).
**Weights:** Operating empty, 70,107 lb (31 800 kg); max fuel load, 32,520 lb (14 750 kg); max payload, 35,715 lb (16 200 kg); max zero fuel, 105,820 lb (48 000 kg); max take-off, 124,560 lb (56 500 kg); max landing, 114,640 lb (52 000 kg).

## DE HAVILLAND CANADA TWIN OTTER

**Country of Origin:** Canada.
**Type:** Commuter and light transport.
**Power Plant:** Two 652 shp (487 kW) Pratt & Whitney PT6A-27 turboprops.
**Performance:** Max cruise, 182 kts (337 km/h) at 10,000 ft (3 050 m); long-range cruise, 145 kts (269 km/h) at 10,000 ft (3 050 m); range with 2,500-lb (1 134-kg) payload, 700 naut mls (1 297 km).
**Accommodation:** Flight crew of one or two and up to 20 passengers seated at 30-in (76-cm) pitch three-abreast.
**Status:** Prototype first flown 20 May 1965; certification May 1966, initial deliveries July 1966. First deliveries of Srs 200, April 1968 and Srs 300, Spring 1969.
**Sales:** Total, more than 820 sold by late 1986, including military and non-airline commercial sales. First 115 aircraft were Series 100, next 115 were Series 200, thereafter Series 300.
**Notes:** As its name suggests, the DHC-6 Twin Otter began life as a twin-engined derivative of the single piston-engined Otter, with which it shares some wing and fuselage components. It has proved to have excellent appeal in the commuter and third-level airline market, with its STOL performance allowing it to bring reliable scheduled service to many close-in town airports. Original Series 100 had shorter nose and Series 300 introduced the uprated PT6A-27 engines. Floatplane, skiplane and amphibious versions are available, and de Havilland has developed a Srs 300M Twin Otter for more specifically military rôles, with wing strong points and provision for a search radar under the nose. This version, and some Srs 300s in civilian but non-airline use, operate at a higher gross weight.

## DE HAVILLAND CANADA TWIN OTTER

**Dimensions:** Span, 65 ft 0 in (19,81 m); length, 51 ft 9 in (15,77 m); height, 19 ft 6 in (5,94 m); wing area, 420 sq ft (39,02 m$^2$).
**Weights:** Operational empty, 7,415 lb (3 363 kg); max payload, 4,280 lb (1 941 kg); max fuel load, 2,583 lb (1 171 kg); max zero fuel, 12,300 lb (5 579 kg); max take-off, 12,500 lb (5 670 kg); max landing, 12,300 lb (5 579 kg).

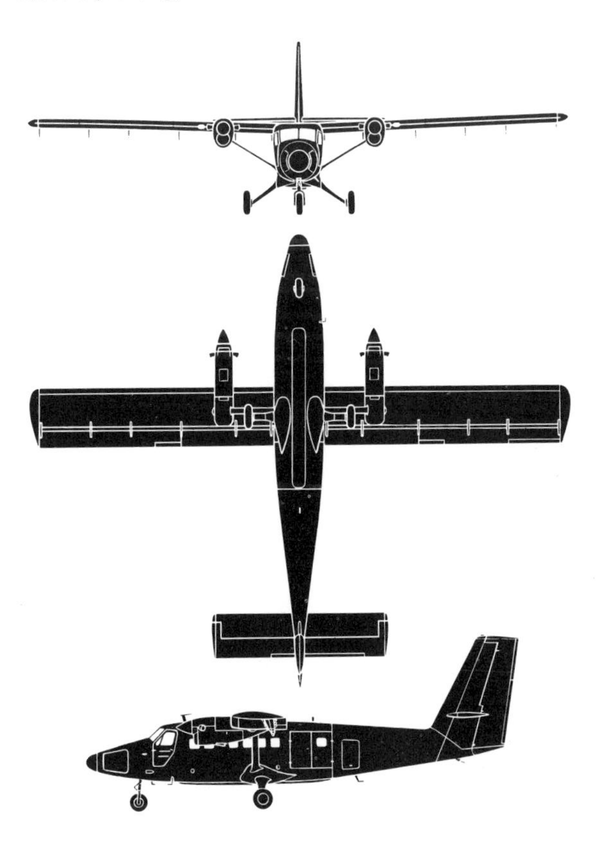

## DE HAVILLAND CANADA DASH 7

**Country of Origin:** Canada.
**Type:** STOL regional airliner.
**Power Plant:** Four 1,120 shp (835 kW) Pratt & Whitney PT6A-50 turboprops.
**Performance:** Max cruise, 227 kts (420 km/h) at 15,000 ft (4 575 m); long-range cruise, 215 kts (399 km/h) at 20,000 ft (6 100 m); range (with 50-passenger payload), 690 naut mls (1 279 km); max range, 1,170 naut mls (2 168 km).
**Accommodation:** Flight crew of two and up to 54 passengers at 29-in (74-cm) pitch four-abreast with central aisle.
**Status:** Two prototypes first flown 27 March and 26 June 1975 respectively. First production aircraft flown 30 May 1977, entered service 3 February 1978 (with Rocky Mountain Airways). Delivery of Srs 150 began in 1986.
**Sales:** Total of 105 sold by early 1987.
**Notes:** The Dash-7 (DHC-7) is among the largest of the regional airliners at present in service, matching the British Aerospace HS.748 and Fokker F27 in capacity but offering STOL performance, which it derives from the use of double slotted flaps operating in the slipstreams from four large-diameter, slow-running four-bladed propellers. Basic aircraft is the Series 100; a few Series 101s are in all-cargo configuration and DHC-7R Ranger is specially equipped for the Canadian Coast Guard. The Srs 150 (and 151 freighter) became available in 1986 and has increased gross weight of 47,000 lb (21 319 kg) and provision for an extra 912 Imp gal (4 154 l) of fuel in wing tanks, increasing range to 2,525 naut mls (4 679 km).

## DE HAVILLAND CANADA DASH 7

**Dimensions:** Span, 93 ft 0 in (28,35 m); length, 80 ft 6 in (24,54 m); height, 26 ft 2 in (7,98 m); wing area, 860 sq ft (79,9 m²).

**Weights:** Operational empty, 27,690 lb (12 560 kg); max fuel, 10,060 lb (4 563 kg); max payload, 11,306 lb (5 127 kg); max zero fuel, 39,000 lb (17 690 kg); max take-off, 44,000 lb (19 958 kg); max landing, 44,000 lb (19 958 kg).

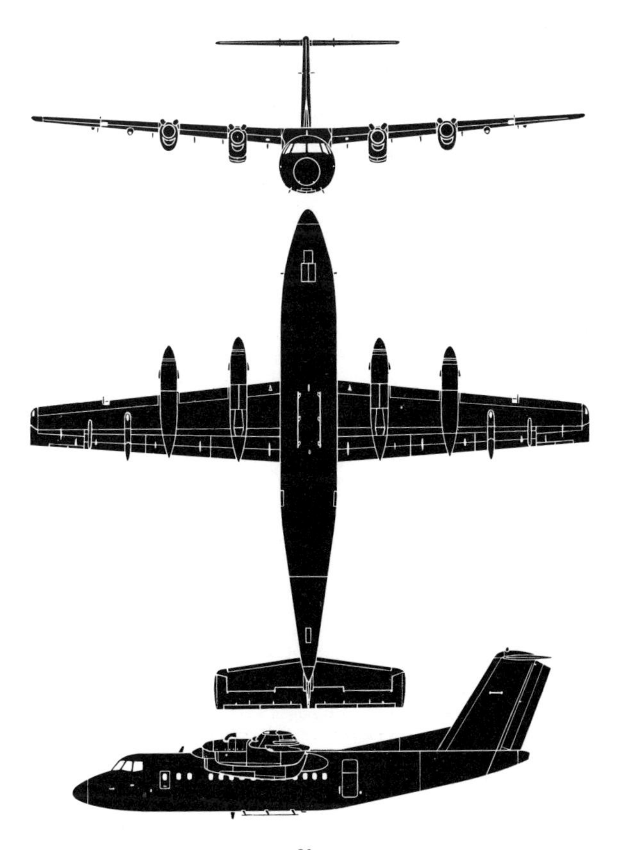

## DE HAVILLAND CANADA DASH 8 SRS 100

**Country of Origin:** Canada.
**Type:** Short-range regional airliner.
**Power Plant:** Two flat-rated 1,800 shp (1 432 kW) Pratt & Whitney PW120A turboprops.
**Performance:** Max cruise, 265 kts (554 km/h) at 25,000 ft (7 620 m); long-range cruise, 237 kts (439 km/h); range with max payload (36 passengers), 1,150 naut mls (2 130 km).
**Accommodation:** Flight crew of two and 36 passengers at 31-in (79-cm) pitch four-abreast with central aisle; maximum, 40.
**Status:** First of four pre-production aircraft flown 20 June 1983, second on 26 October 1983. Canadian certification on 28 September 1984. First delivery 23 October 1984.
**Sales:** Total Dash 8 sales including options, 194 by end-1986, of which 115 orders and 41 options for the Srs 100.
**Notes:** The Dash 8 (DHC-8) is the latest in the Canadian company's successful series of small transports with special STOL capabilities. It was designed to serve as a junior partner with the Dash 7, with which it shares a similar configuration, featuring a high wing and T-tail. Like the larger aircraft, the Dash 8 depends upon large-area trailing edge flaps and a sophisticated control system for its low-speed performance and control, without the use of leading-edge flaps. Intended primarily for use by the regional airlines, the Dash 8 is also offered in executive versions, and with mixed passenger/cargo layouts including quick-change options. The entire accommodation area is pressurized and provision is made for single-pilot operation. The Srs 300, which features a lengthened fuselage and uprated engines, is described separately.

# DE HAVILLAND CANADA DASH 8 SRS 100

**Dimensions:** Span, 85 ft 0 in (25,91 m); length, 73 ft 0 in (22,25 m); height, 24 ft 7 in (7,49 m); wing area, 585 sq ft (54,30 m²).
**Weights:** Operating weight empty, 21,590 lb (9 793 kg); standard fuel weight, 5,678 lb (2 576 kg); max payload, 7,824 lb (3 549 kg); max zero fuel, 31,000 lb (14 062 kg); max take-off, 34,500 lb (15 649 kg); max landing, 33,900 lb (14 923 kg).

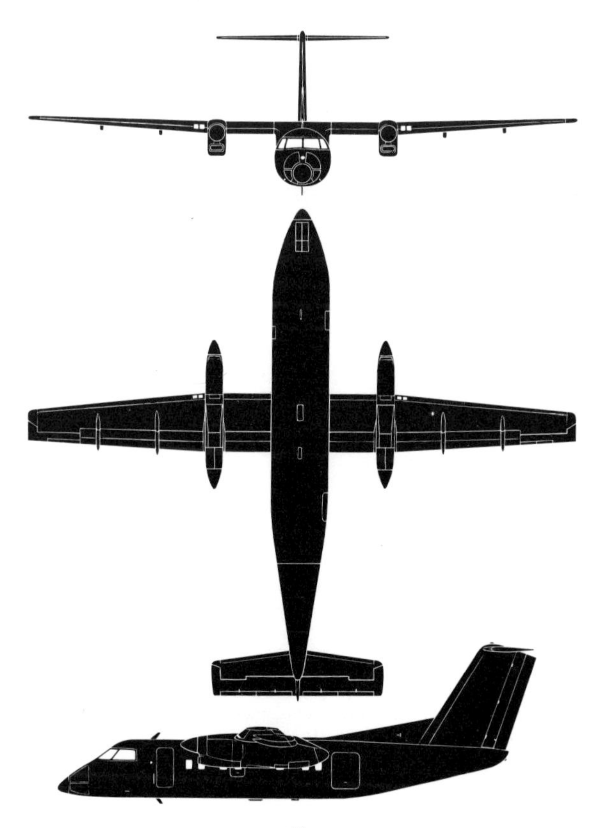

## DE HAVILLAND CANADA DASH 8 SRS 300

**Country of Origin:** Canada.
**Type:** Short-range regional airliner.
**Power Plant:** Two 2,380 shp (1 776 kW) Pratt & Whitney PW123 turboprops.
**Performance:** Max cruising speed, 285 kts (528 km/h) at 15,000 ft (4 570 m); range with 50-passenger payload, 800 naut mls (1 482 km); range with max fuel, 2,050 naut mls (3 800 km).
**Accommodation:** Flight crew of two and up to 56 passengers four-abreast with single aisle at 29-in (74-cm) pitch; typical layout for 50 passengers at 32-in (81-cm) pitch.
**Status:** Full-scale development confirmed during 1986, with modification of a Srs 100 to serve as the first prototype, for first flight May 1987. Two additional aircraft for flight development to fly later in 1987, to achieve Canadian and US certification in June 1988. First customer delivery September 1988.
**Sales:** Total of 23 firm sales and 12 options by early 1987.
**Notes:** The successful entry into service of the Dash 8 Srs 100 (see previous pages) in 1985 led de Havilland to study a number of possible derivative models. These included an increased gross weight option for the Srs 100 itself, as well as corporate and military variants; in addition, a possible stretch of the basic aircraft began to be seriously studied. Although the 50/56-seat Dash 7 was already in production, a Dash 8 enlarged to offer similar capacity offered more attractive economics, since it used only two engines. Following the acquisition of de Havilland by Boeing early in 1986 whereupon it became a subsidiary of Boeing of Canada Ltd, the market prospects for the Dash 300 were endorsed and development proceeded to the time scale indicated above.

## DE HAVILLAND CANADA DASH 8 SRS 300

**Dimensions:** Span, 90 ft 0 in (27,43 m); length, 84 ft 3 in (25,68 m); height, 24 ft 7 in (7,49 m); wing area, 605 sq ft (56,20 m$^2$).

**Weights:** Operating weight empty, 24,700 lb (11 204 kg); max payload, 12,500 lb (5 670 kg); max fuel, 5,678 lb (2 576 kg); max take-off, 41,000 lb (18 643 kg); max landing, 40,000 lb (18 145 kg).

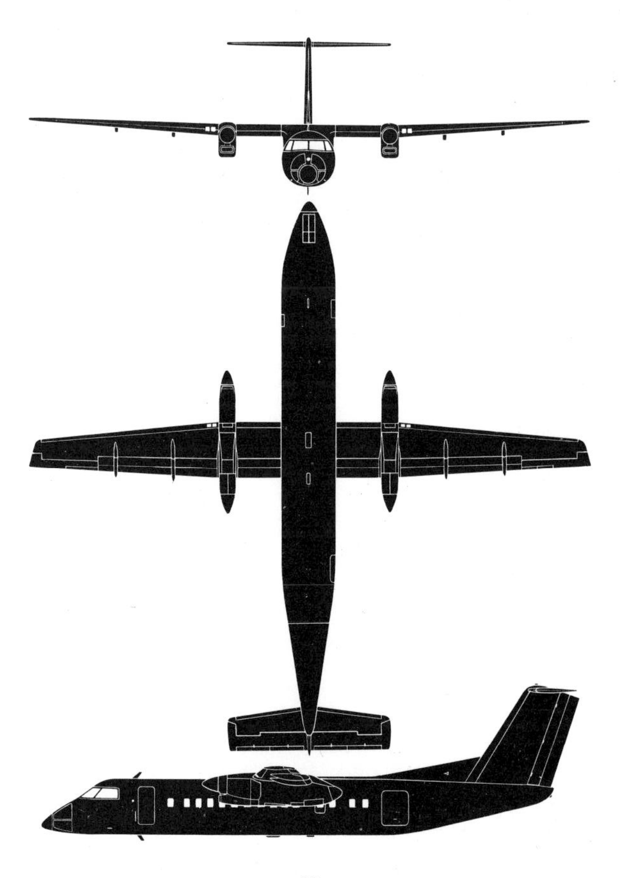

## DORNIER 228

**Country of Origin:** Federal Germany. **Type:** Commuter airliner.
**Power Plant:** Two flat-rated 715 shp (533 kW) Garrett TPE 331-5-252D turboprops.
**Performance:** (Do 228–200) Max cruise, 199 kts (370 km/h) at sea level, 231 kts (428 km/h) at 10,000 ft (3 050 m); max payload range (19 passengers), 323 naut mls (600 km); range with max fuel, 1,460 naut mls (2 704 km).
**Accommodation:** Flight crew of two and (–100) 15 or (–200) 19 passengers at 30-in (76-cm) pitch, two-abreast with central aisle.
**Status:** The prototypes of the Do 228-100 and -200 flew respectively on 28 March and 9 May 1981, and were certificated on 18 December 1981 and 6 September 1982 respectively. Deliveries of the Srs 100 (to A/S Norving) began in February 1982. Deliveries from the Hindustan Aeronautics assembly line at Kanpur (to Vayudoot) began 22 March 1986.
**Sales:** Firm orders for the two versions of the Do 228 totalled approximately 110 by the beginning of 1987. Sales about equally divided between Series 100 and Series 200.
**Notes:** Mating a new-technology wing of supercritical section with the fuselage cross section of the utility Do 128 and a retractable nosewheel undercarriage, the Do 228 is manufactured in two versions, the -100 and -200, these differing only dimensionally in length. This unpressurised regional airliner and utility aircraft has large-span single-slotted Fowler flaps and flaperons. Hindustan Aeronautics has a licence to build about 150 Dornier 228s for military and civil use in India.

## DORNIER 228

**Dimensions:** Span, 55 ft 8 in (16,97 m); length (-100), 49 ft 4 in (15,04 m), (-200), 54 ft 3 in (16,55 m); height, 15 ft 11¼ in (4,86 m); wing area, 344.46 sq ft (32,00 $m^2$).
**Weights:** Operating weight empty, 7,820 lb (3 547 kg); max payload, 4,394 lb (1 993 kg); max zero fuel, 11,900 lb (5 400 kg); max take-off, 12,570 lb (5 700 kg); max landing, 12,570 lb (5 700 kg).

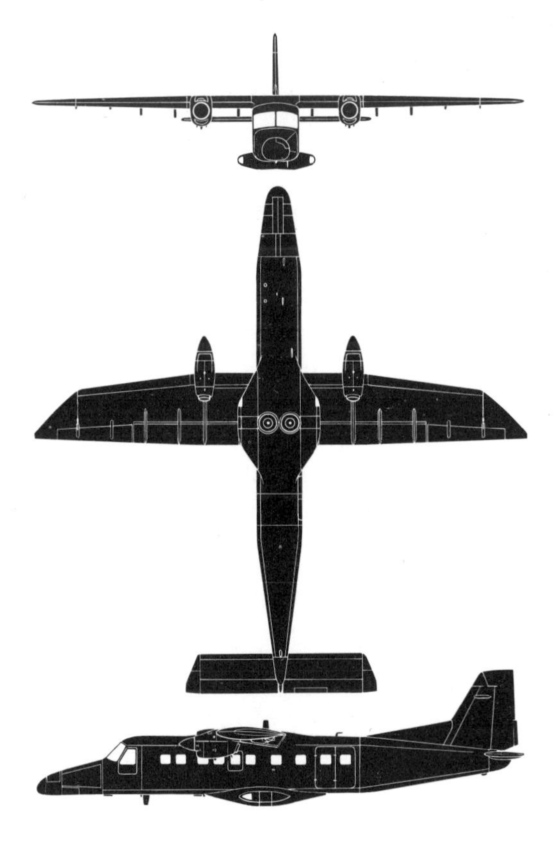

## DOUGLAS DC-3

**Country of Origin:** USA.
**Type:** Short-range passenger and freight transport.
**Power Plant:** Two 1,200 shp Pratt & Whitney R-1830-92 Twin Wasp air-cooled radial engines.
**Performance** (Typical commercial operation, post-war): Max speed, 187 kts (346 km/h); economical cruise, 143 kts (266 km/h) at 6,000 ft (1 830 m); range with max payload, 305 naut mls (563 km); range with max fuel, 1,312 naut mls (2 430 km).
**Accommodation:** Flight crew of two; typical passenger layout provides for 28–32, four-abreast at up to 38-in (96.5-cm) pitch with central aisle.
**Status:** DST (prototype for DC-3 series) first flown 17 December 1935; first service use (American Airlines) 25 June 1936. Production completed 1946.
**Sales:** Total of 10,655 built, including 430 for commercial customers prior to December 1941, 10,197 for military use before and during World War II and 28 assembled post-war from surplus components as DC-3Ds. About 350 were still in airline service at the end of 1986.
**Notes:** The DC-3 established an outstanding reputation in the five years before the USA entered World War II, as the most efficient and comfortable short-medium range airliner then available. Adopted for military use, it gained more fame as the C-47 Skytrain and the Dakota, and many thousands were civilianized after the war ended to provide the backbone of the air transport industry in the early post war years. They have proved almost indestructible, and still in 1987 play a part in the air transport system of many nations, especially in the Third World.

## DOUGLAS DC-3

**Dimensions:** Span, 95 ft 0 in (28,96 m); length, 64 ft 6 in (19,66 m); height, 16 ft 11½ in (5,16 m); wing area, 987 sq ft (91,7 m²).
**Weights:** Typical operating weight empty, 17,720 lb (8 030 kg); max payload, 6,600 lb (2 994 kg); max fuel, 4,820 lb (2 186 kg); max take-off, 28,000 lb (12 700 kg); max landing, 26,900 lb (12 202 kg).

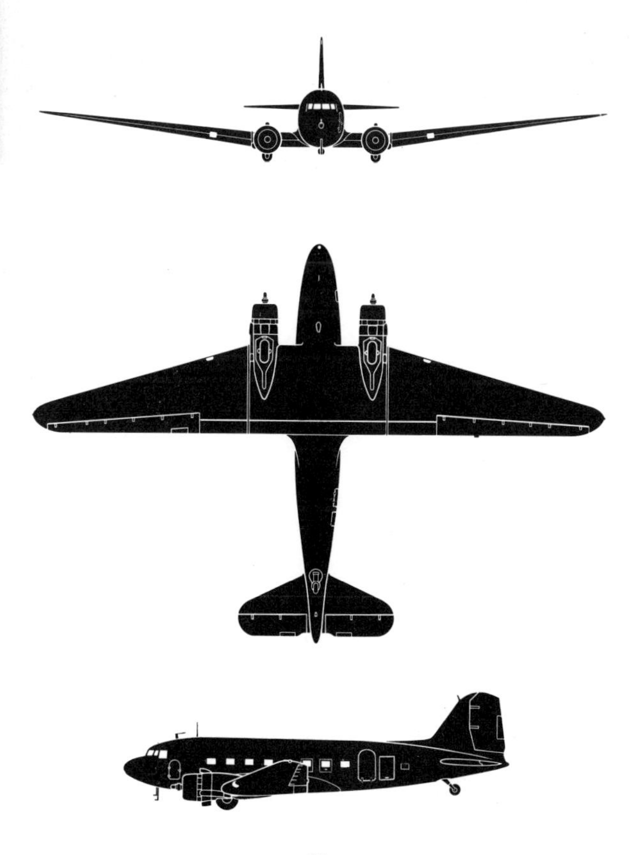

# DOUGLAS DC-6 (AND DC-7)

**Country of Origin:** USA.
**Type:** Medium to long-range passenger and freight transport.
**Power Plant:** Four 2,400 hp (1 790 kW) Pratt & Whitney R-2800-CA-15 air-cooled radial engines.
**Performance:** Max cruising speed, 275 kts (509 km/h); typical economical cruise, 243 kts (451 km/h) at 16,000 ft (4 877 m) at mean weight of 83,000 lb (37 650 kg); range with max payload, 1,650 naut mls (3 058 km); range with max fuel, 2,320 naut mls (4 300 km).
**Accommodation:** Flight crew of three or four; typically 68–86 passengers five-abreast with offset aisle; maximum, 102.
**Status:** Prototype (military XC-112) first flown 15 February 1946; first production DC-6 flown June 1946, first airline service (United) 17 April 1947. DC-6A first flown 29 September 1949, entered service (Slick) 16 April 1951; DC-6B first flown 2 February 1951, entered service (American) 29 April 1951. DC-7 first flown 18 May 1953, entered service (American) 29 November 1953; DC-7B first flown 25 April 1955, entered service (Pan American) 23 May 1955; DC-7C first flown 20 December 1955, entered service (Pan American) 1 June 1956. Production completed (DC-6) February 1959 (DC-7) December 1958.
**Sales:** Total of 1,042 DC-6/7 variants built, including 174 DC-6, 73 DC-6A, 288 DC-6B, 168 Military, 106 DC-7, 112 DC-7B and 121 DC-7C.
**Notes:** DC-6 and DC-7, in their successive sub-variants, were progressive extrapolations of the DC-4, with same configuration but various fuselage lengths. About 60 DC-6s were still in commercial service at the beginning of 1987, but scarcely any DC-7s were then surviving.

## DOUGLAS DC-6B

**Dimensions:** Span, 117 ft 6 in (35,81 m); length, 105 ft 7 in (32,2 m); height, 29 ft 3 in (8,92 m); wing area, 1,463 sq ft (135,9 m²).
**Weights:** Operating weight, empty, about 62,000 lb (28 123 kg); max payload, 24,565 lb (11 143 kg); max fuel, 32,950 lb (14 946 kg); max zero fuel, 83,200 lb (37 740 kg); max take-off, 107,000 lb (48 534 kg); max landing, 88,200 lb (40 007 kg).

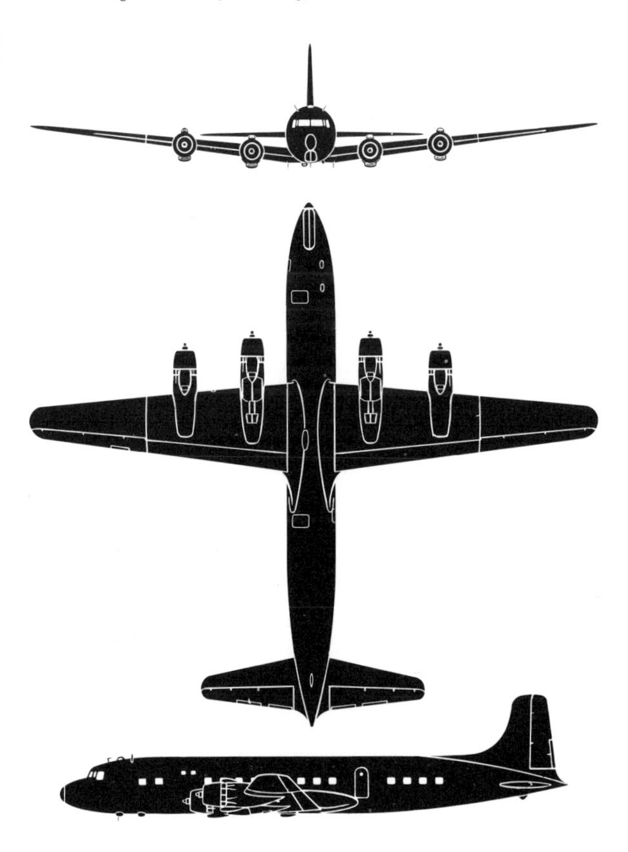

## EMBRAER EMB-110 BANDEIRANTE

**Country of Origin:** Brazil.
**Type:** Regional airliner.
**Power Plant:** Two flat-rated 750 shp (560 kW) Pratt & Whitney PT6A-34 turboprops.
**Performance:** Max cruise, 221 kts (410 km/h) at 10,000 ft (3 050 m); long-range cruise 181 kts (356 km/h) at 10,000 ft (3 050 m); may payload (19 passengers) range, (P1) 200 kts (370 km); range with max fuel, 1,060 naut mls (1 964 km).
**Accommodation:** Flight crew of two and up to 18 passengers three-abreast at 31-in (79-cm) pitch.
**Status:** Military prototypes first flown 26 October 1968, 19 October 1969 and 26 June 1970; first production EMB-110 flown 9 August 1972; first airline use (15-seat EMB-110C) 16 April 1973. Stretched EMB-110P2 first flown 3 May 1977. Production rate, approx six a month.
**Sales:** Total EMB-110 deliveries (military and civil) nearly 500, including more than 300 for commercial use.
**Notes:** The unpressurized Bandeirante originated to a Brazilian military specification as the first substantial aircraft design and production programme undertaken wholly in Brazil. EMB-110P2 is basic all-passenger (up to 21) version, P1 has larger rear-loading door for passenger/cargo convertible operations. Original certification basis for the commercial Bandeirante was FAR-23 at 12,500 lb (5 670 kg) gross weight; the recertificated EMB-110/41 (to SFAR 41) operates at weights quoted here. Commencing with the 439th aircraft in 1983, a number of refinements were introduced, including dihedral on the tailplane, resulting in the designations EMB-110P1A, -110P1A/41, -110P2A and -110P2A/41.

## EMBRAER EMB-110 BANDEIRANTE

**Dimensions:** Span, 50 ft $3\frac{1}{2}$ in (15,33 m); length, 49 ft $6\frac{1}{2}$ in (15,10 m); height 16 ft $1\frac{3}{4}$ in (4,92 m); wing area, 313.23 sq ft (29,10 $m^2$).
**Weights:** Operational empty (P2) 8,565 lb (3 855 kg); max fuel weight, 2,883 lb (1 308 kg); max payload (P2), 3,443 lb (1 561 kg); max zero fuel, 12,015 lb (5 450 kg); max take-off, 13,010 lb (5 900 kg); max landing, 12,566 lb (5 700 kg).

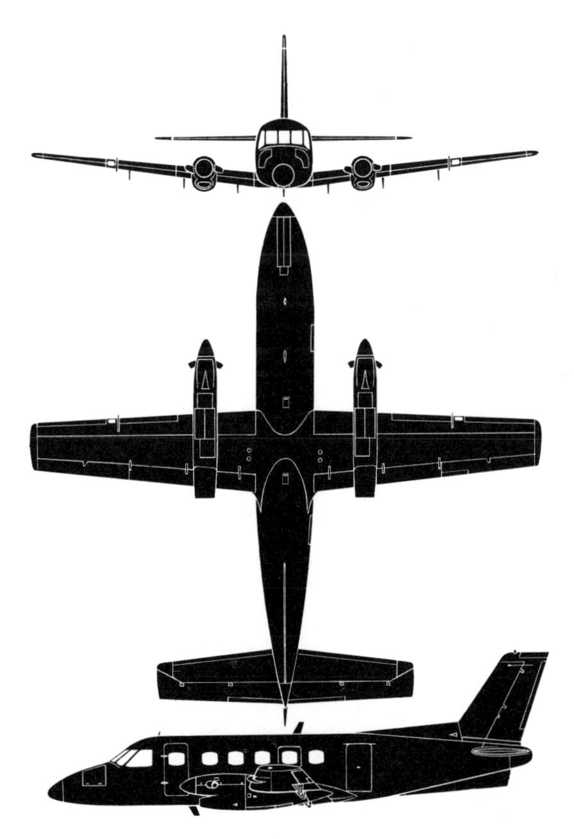

## EMBRAER EMB-120 BRASILIA

**Country of Origin:** Brazil.
**Type:** Regional airliner.
**Power Plant:** Two 1,800 shp (1 343 kW) Pratt & Whitney Canada PW118 turboprops.
**Performance:** Max cruise, 300 kts (556 km/h) at 22,000 ft (6 705 m); long-range cruise, 260 kts (482 km/h) at 25,000 ft (7 620 m); max payload range (30 passengers), 945 naut mls (1 750 km) at econ cruise; max fuel range, 1,610 naut mls (2 982 km).
**Accommodation:** Flight crew of two and 30 passengers at 31-in (79-cm) pitch three-abreast with offset aisle. Optional arrangements for 24 and 26 passengers with enlarged baggage compartment.
**Status:** First Brasilia entered flight test on 27 July 1983, second on 21 December and third on 9 May 1984. Certification in Brazil on 16 May 1985 and in USA on 9 July 1985. First production delivery (to ASA) August 1985.
**Sales:** Approximately 70 aircraft on firm orders by early 1987, plus some 80 on option.
**Notes:** Design work on the EMB-120 Brasilia was launched in September 1979, the structural design having been finalised in January 1982. Corporate transport and all-cargo versions are available and proposed versions include military models for maritime surveillance, aeromedical evacuation, electronic intelligence, paratroop transportation and search and rescue. Initial aircraft were powered by the 1,500 shp (1 120 kW) PW115 engines, a switch being made to the more powerful PW118 or PW118A in 1986.

## EMBRAER EMB-120 BRASILIA

**Dimensions:** Span, 64 ft 10¾ in (19,78 m); length 65 ft 7 in (20,00 m); height, 20 ft 10 in (6,35 m); wing area, 424.46 sq ft (39,43 $m^2$).
**Weights:** Operational empty, 15,163 lb (6 878 kg); max fuel weight, 5,510 lb (2 500 kg); max payload, 7,650 lb (3 470 kg); max zero fuel, 23,148 lb (10 500 kg); max take-off 25,353 lb (11 500 kg); max landing, 24,802 lb (11 250 kg).

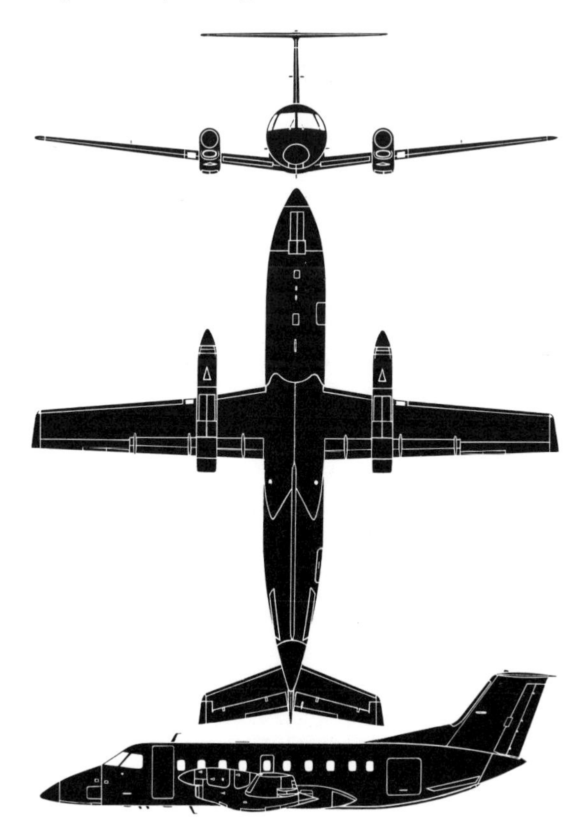

## FAIRCHILD F-27 AND FH-227

**Country of Origin:** USA.
**Type:** Short-range turboprop transport.
**Power Plant** (FH-227): Two 2,230 eshp (1 664 kW) Rolls-Royce Dart 532-7 or (FH-227D, E) 2,300 eshp (1 716 kW) Dart 532-7L turboprop engines.
**Performance** (FH-227E): Max cruising speed, 255 kts (473 km/h) at 15,000 ft (4 570 m); best economy cruise, 236 kts (435 km/h) at 25,000 ft (7 620 m); range with max payload, 570 naut mls (1 055 km); range with max fuel, 1,440 naut mls (2 660 km).
**Accommodation:** Flight crew of two (optionally, three) and up to 52 passengers four-abreast with central aisle at 31-in (79-cm) pitch, or a maximum of 56.
**Status:** Prototype Fairchild-built F27s flown 12 April and 23 May 1958; FAA certification 16 July 1958, entered service (West Coast Airlines) 27 September 1958. First FH-227 flown 27 January 1966; entered service (Mohawk) mid-1966. Production completed December 1968.
**Sales:** Fairchild built 128 F27s, plus a complete rebuild of first prototype after accidental damage, and 78 of the lengthened-fuselage FH-227s.
**Notes:** Fairchild acquired a licence to build the Fokker F27 (see separate entry) on 26 April 1956 and put the aircraft into production at the same time as the parent company, actually achieving first deliveries and airline service before Fokker's own Friendships. Variants up to F-27M were built or projected, all with the same basic dimensions and varying Dart models. Fairchild also was first to develop a stretched variant, as the FH-227, nearly two years before Fokker flew the first Mk 500, with slightly less 'stretch'.

## FAIRCHILD FH-227

**Dimensions:** Span, 95 ft 2 in (29,00 m); length, 83 ft 8 in (25,50 m); height, 27 ft 7 in (8,41 m); wing area, 754 sq ft (70,0 m$^2$).
**Weights:** Operating weight empty, 22,923 lb (10 398 kg); max payload, 11,200 lb (5 080 kg); max fuel, 8,920 lb (4 046 kg); max zero fuel, 41,000 lb (18 600 kg); max take-off, 45,500 lb (20 639 kg); max landing, 45,000 lb (20 412 kg).

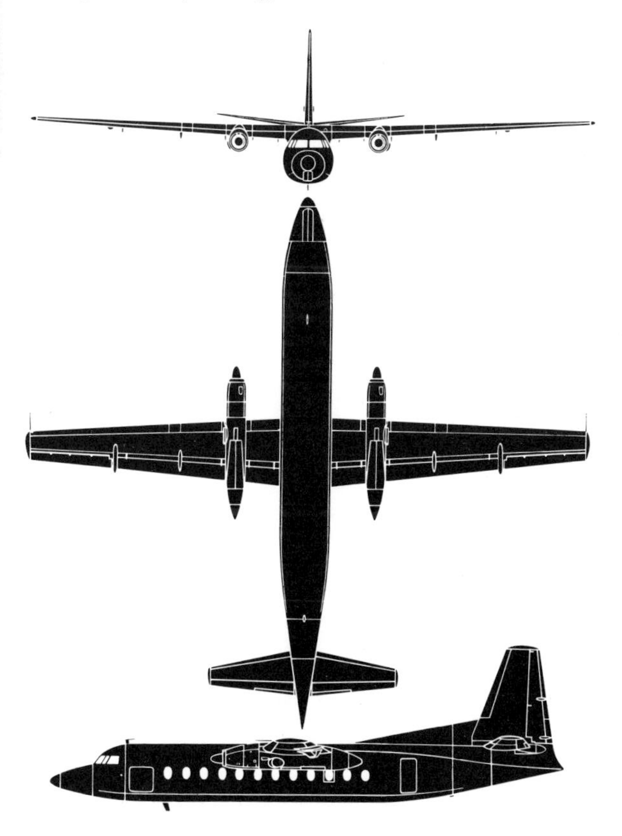

# FAIRCHILD METRO III

**Country of Origin:** USA.
**Type:** Commuter airliner.
**Power Plant:** Two (Metro III) 1,000 shp (746 kW) Garrett TPE331-11U-611G turboprops, or (Metro IIIA) 1,100 shp (820 kW) Pratt & Whitney PT6A-45R turboprops.
**Performance:** (Metro III) Max cruise, 278 kts (515 km/h) at 12,500 ft (3 810 m); long-range cruise, 256 kts (475 km/h) at 25,000 ft (7 620 m); max payload range (19 passengers), 869 kts (1 612 km) at cost econ cruise.
**Accommodation:** Flight crew of two and 19 passengers at 30-in (76-cm) pitch two-abreast with central aisle.
**Status:** Metro prototype first flown 26 August 1969; certification 11 June 1970. Customer deliveries began 1973 (Air Wisconsin). Metro II introduced 1974; Metro IIA certificated to SFAR-41 23 June 1980. Metro III entered service 1981. Metro IIIA first flown 31 December 1981. Metro production rate averaged four monthly during 1986.
**Sales:** Approximately 350 Metros of all versions delivered by the beginning of 1987.
**Notes:** Metro III differs from earlier Metros in having a new, longer-span wing and more efficient engines, and Metro IIIA marks first use of Pratt & Whitney engines in this family of commuter aircraft. Both are certificated to SFAR-41B at weights shown above. The name Expediter applies to an all cargo version of the Metro III, with increased payload. Earlier Metro I and Metro II were limited to 12,500 lb (5 670 kg) gross weight by FAR Part 23 regulations. The name Merlin is used for variants of the basic Metro design furnished for corporate/business use. An improved corporate variant known as the Fairchild 400 was built only as a prototype.

## FAIRCHILD METRO III

**Dimensions:** Span, 57 ft 0 in (17,37 m); length, 59 ft $4\frac{1}{4}$ in (18,09 m); height, 16 ft 8 in (5,08 m); wing area, 309 sq ft (28,71 m²).
**Weights:** Operational empty (III) 8,737 lb (3 963 kg), (IIIA), 8,823 lb (4 022 kg); max payload (III), 4,880 lb (2 214 kg); max zero fuel (III & IIIA), 12,500 lb (5 670 kg); max take-off (III & IIIA), 14,500 lb (6 577 kg); max landing (III & IIIA), 14,000 lb (6 350 kg).

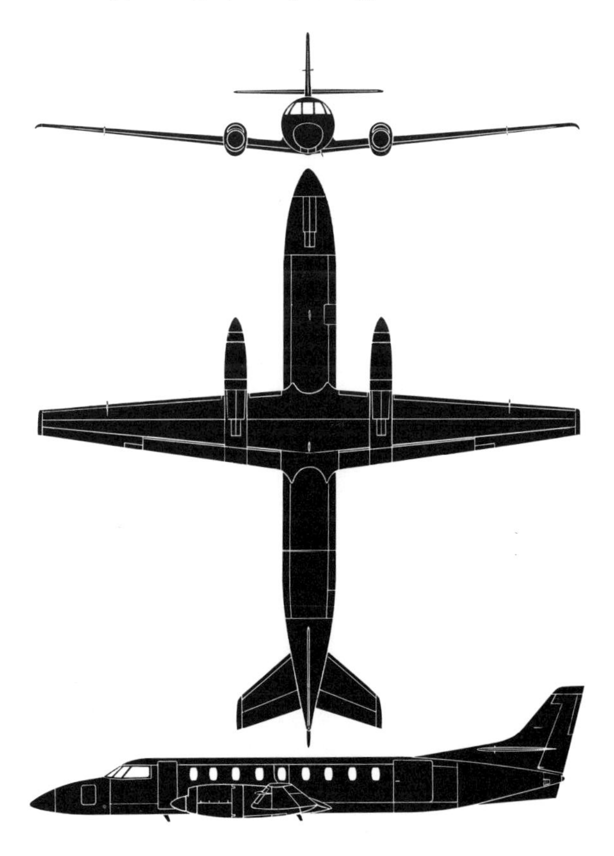

## FOKKER F27

**Country of Origin:** Netherlands.
**Type:** Short-range turboprop transport.
**Power Plant:** Two 2,280 ehp (1 700 kW) Rolls-Royce Dart 552 turboprops.
**Performance:** Max cruise at 38,000-lb (17 237-kg) weight 259 kts (480 km/h) at 20,000 ft (6 100 m); long-range cruise, 232 kts (430 km/h) at 20,000 ft (6 100 m): range with max payload 1,285 naut mls (2 070 km); range with max fuel, 1,374 naut mls (2 211 km).
**Accommodation:** Flight crew of two (optionally, three) and up to 44 passengers four-abreast with central aisle at 30-in (76-cm) pitch.
**Status:** Two F27 prototypes first flown 24 November 1955 and 29 January 1957 respectively; US certification, 29 October 1957. First production F27 flown 23 March 1958; entered service (Mk 100 with Aer Lingus) 15 December 1958. Mk 200 first flown 20 September 1959; Mk 500 first flown 15 November 1967; Mk 600 first flown 28 November 1968.
**Sales:** Total of 581 F27s built by Fokker (and 205 by Fairchild as described separately), including about 200 military/government agency and corporate. Totals include 85 Mk 100, 138 Mk 200, 13 Mk 300, 218 Mk 400/600, 112 Mk 500 and 15 Maritime. Production ended in 1986 with two F27s for the Royal Thai Navy.
**Notes:** Fokker F27 is the best-selling turboprop airliner to date (excluding Soviet types possibly built in larger numbers). Current versions are Mk 200, Mk 400 (primarily military) and Mk 500 (longer fuselage). The original Mk 100 had RDa6 engines, as did the Mk 300 Combiplane with side-loading freight door. The Fokker 50 is described separately on the next pages.

## FOKKER F27 FRIENDSHIP Mk 200

**Dimensions:** Span, 95 ft 2 in (29,00 m); length, 77 ft 3½ in (23,56 m); height, 27 ft 10¾ in (8,50 m); wing area, 754 sq ft (70,0 m²).
**Weights:** Operating empty, 24,600 lb (11 159 kg); max payload, 10,340 lb (4 690 kg); max internal fuel, 13,180 lb (5 980 kg); max zero fuel, 39,500 lb (17,917 kg); max take-off, 45,000 lb (20 412 kg); max landing, 41,000 lb (18 598 kg).

## FOKKER 50

**Country of Origin:** Netherlands
**Type:** Short-range regional turboprop transport.
**Power Plant:** Two 2,150 shp (1 603 kW) Pratt & Whitney PW124 turboprops.
**Performance:** Max cruising speed, 278 kts (515 km/h) at 21,000 ft (6400 m); long-range cruising speed, 245 kts (454 km/h) at 25,000 ft (7 620 m); range with 50-passenger payload, 750 naut mls (1 390 km) at standard weight, 1,610 naut mls (2 983 km) at optional high weight.
**Accommodation:** Flight crew of two and up to 58 passengers four-abreast with single aisle at 30-in (76-cm) pitch; standard layout for 50 passengers.
**Status:** Prototypes converted from Fokker F27 airframes flown on 28 December 1985 and 30 April 1986. Production deliveries commencing early 1987, to Ansett Transport Industries.
**Sales:** Total of 39 firm sales and 12 options by early 1987.
**Notes:** After studying a number of possible derivative versions of the F27 Friendship, Fokker announced in November 1983 its intention to proceed with development and production of this re-engined variant, named the Fokker 50 in line with its passenger capacity. The major innovation was to use Pratt & Whitney PW124 engines in place of Rolls-Royce Darts, but the Fokker 50 also has a number of other changes, with only some 20 per cent of components common with those of the F27. Among system changes is the use of hydraulics for undercarriage and flap operation. A larger number of small cabin windows aids flexibility of layout, and small surfaces at the wing tips are known as 'Foklets'.

## FOKKER 50

**Dimensions:** Span, 95 ft 1¾ in (29,00 m); length, 82 ft 10 in (25,25 m); height, 28 ft 7 in (8,60 m); wing area, 754 sq ft (70,0 m²).
**Weights:** Operating weight empty, 27,850 lb (12 633 kg); max payload, 12,700 lb (5 760 kg); max fuel, 9,090 lb (4 123 kg); max take-off, 41,865 lb (18 990 kg); optional high gross weight, 45,900 lb (20 820 kg); max landing, 41,865 lb (18 990 kg); optional high landing weight, 43,500 lb (19 731 kg).

## FOKKER F28

**Country of Origin:** Netherlands.
**Type:** Regional jet airliner.
**Power Plant:** Two 9,900 lb st (4 490 kgp) Rolls-Royce RB.183-2 Mk 555-15P turbofans.
**Performance:** (Mk 4000 at 63,934 lb/29 000 kg gross weight): Max cruising speed, 436 kts (808 km/h) at 33,000 ft (10 058 m); long-range cruise, 354 kts (656 km/h) at 30,000 ft (9 150 m); range with max payload (85 passengers), long-range cruise, 1,125 naut mls (2 085 km).
**Accommodation:** Flight crew of two; max one-class seating for 85 passengers, five-abreast, at 29-in (74-cm) pitch.
**Status:** Prototypes first flown on 9 May and 3 August 1967 respectively; pre-production standard F28 flown 20 October 1967. Certification and first delivery (to LTU) 24 February 1969. Mk 6000 prototype flown 27 September 1973, not produced. First Mk 4000 long-fuselage variant flown 20 October 1976.
**Sales:** Total of 241 F28s sold (including military) to more than 50 operators by the end of 1986, when production ended.
**Notes:** F28 was developed and put into production as Fokker's first jet transport, to complement the highly successful F27 turboprop twin. The Mk 4000, for which data are given here, is of particular interest to regional airlines, and has been sold to such operators in the USA, the Far East, Africa and Europe. The Mk 2000, no longer in production, has the same fuselage length, Mk 1000 and Mk 3000 have a length of 43 ft 0 in (13,10 m) and up to 65 passengers. The Mks 5000 and 6000 were similar to the Mks 3000 and 4000 respectively, with leading-edge slats. The re-engined and stretched Fokker 100 is described separately on the next pages.

## FOKKER F28 FELLOWSHIP

**Dimensions:** Span, 82 ft 3 in (25,07 m); length, 97 ft 1¾ in (29,61 m); height, 27 ft 9½ in (8,47 m); wing area, 850 sq ft (79,00 m²).
**Weights:** Operating empty, 38,683 lb (17 546 kg); max payload, 23,317 lb (10 576 kg); standard fuel, 17,240 lb (7 820 kg); max fuel, 23,080 lb (10 469 kg); max zero fuel, 62,000 lb (28 122 kg); max take-off, 73,000 lb (33 110 kg); max landing; 69,500 lb (31 524 kg).

## FOKKER 100

**Country of Origin:** Netherlands.
**Type:** Short-to-medium range regional jet transport.
**Power Plant:** Two 13,850 lb st (6 282 kgp) Rolls-Royce Tay Mk 620-15 turbofans.
**Performance:** Max cruising speed, 432 kts (800 km/h) at 35,000 ft (10 670 m); long-range cruising speed, 404 kts (747 km/h) at 35,000 ft (10 670 m); range with max passenger payload, 1,200 naut mls (2 224 km).
**Accommodation:** Flight crew of two and up to 119 passengers five-abreast with single aisle at 29-in (74-cm) pitch; typical mixed-class payout for 12 first-class and 85 economy class.
**Status:** First prototype flown 30 November 1986. First customer deliveries late 1987.
**Sales:** Total of 89 firm sales and 91 options by early 1987.
**Notes:** For several years, Fokker conducted intensive design studies and evaluations of small-capacity, short-range airliners for the regional portion of the market. For the most part, these studies were based on the Fokker F28 (see previous pages) and they embraced possible collaboration with other companies, especially McDonnell Douglas. Finally, in November 1983, Fokker announced that it was going ahead with the Fokker 100 as a private venture, aided by Netherlands government funding and with participation by other companies already contributing to the F28. Differences, other than the complete updating of the interior, flight deck and systems, are the use of Tay engines in place of Speys (from which the Tay is derived, with a new LP system) and an 18 ft 10 in stretch of the fuselage. A high gross weight version, at 95,000 lb (43 090 kg), will have 15,100 lb st (6 850 kgp) Tay 650s.

## FOKKER 100

**Dimensions:** Span, 92 ft $1\frac{1}{2}$ in (28,08 m); length, 115 ft $10\frac{1}{4}$ in (35,31 m); height, 27 ft $10\frac{1}{2}$ in (8,50 m); wing area, 1,014.7 sq ft (94,30 m²).
**Weights:** Operating weight empty, 51,260 lb (23 250 kg); max payload, 25,353 lb (11 500 kg); max fuel, 23,070 lb (10 460 kg); max take-off, 91,500 lb (41 500 kg); max landing, 84,500 lb (38 330 kg).

## GAF NOMAD 22 AND 24

**Country of Origin:** Australia.
**Type:** Commuter airliner and general utility light transport.
**Power Plant:** Two flat-rated 420 shp (313 kW) Allison 250-B-17C turboprops.
**Performance:** (N22B) Max cruise, 165 kts (311 km/h) at 10,000 ft (3 050 m); long-range cruise, 140 kts (260 km/h) at 10,000 ft (3 050 m); max payload range (16 passengers), 580 naut mls (1074 km) at 258 kts (297 km/h).
**Accommodation:** Flight crew of two and up to (N22B) 12 or (N24A) 16 passengers in single seats arranged each side of central aisle at 29-in (74-cm) pitch.
**Status:** Two N22 prototypes flown 23 July and 5 December 1971 respectively. First production N22 flown 3 October 1974 and certificated 29 April 1975 (with FAA certification on 20 May 1977). First service 18 December 1975 (with Aero Pelican). First stretched N24 flown 17 December 1975 and certificated October 1977.
**Sales:** Total of 170 built, including all versions, about half of these for commercial use, principally small airlines in Australia and Pacific territories, plus a few N24 Commuterliners in the USA.
**Notes:** The Nomad is notable for its STOL performance and its Australian origin. It has sold in several military versions as well as for airline and specialised commercial use. N22B and N24A differ principally in length, as indicated above. One N22B has been flown with amphibious floats. Production ended in 1984, but in May 1985 the N22B was recertificated at the increased gross weight of 8,950 lb (4 060 kg), as the N22C.

## GAF NOMAD 22 AND 24

**Dimensions:** Span, 54 ft 2 in (16,51 m); length (N22B), 41 ft $2\frac{1}{2}$ in (12,57 m), (N24A), 47 ft 1 in (14,35 m); height, 18 ft $1\frac{1}{2}$ in (5,52 m); wing area, 324 sq ft (30,10 m$^2$).

**Weights:** (N22B) Operational empty, 5,436 lb (2 466 kg); max payload, 3,714 lb (1 685 kg); max usable fuel, 2,350 lb (1 066 kg); max zero fuel, 8,250 lb (3 742 kg); max take-off, 8,500 lb (3 855 kg); max landing, 8,500 lb (3 855 kg).

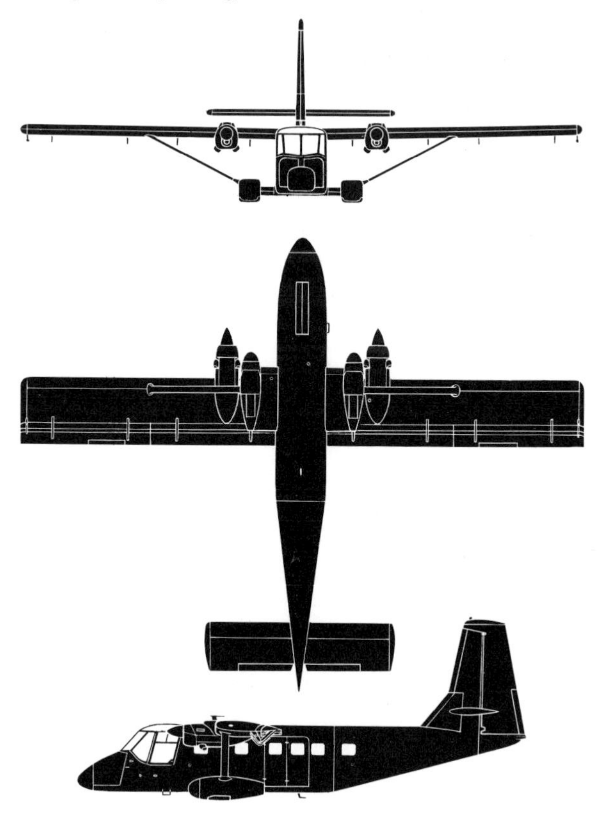

## GRUMMAN GULFSTREAM I

**Country of Origin:** USA.
**Type:** Short-to-medium range small-capacity commuterliner.
**Power Plant:** Two 1,990 shp (1 484 kW) Rolls-Royce Dart 529-8X or -8E turboprops.
**Performance:** Max cruising speed, 302 kts (560 km/h) at 25,000 ft (7 625 m); best economy cruising speed, 250 kts (463 km/h) at 25,000 ft (7 625 m); range with max fuel, 2,540 naut mls (4 088 km) with 2,740-lb (1 243-kg) pay-load.
**Accommodation:** Flight crew of two and up to 24 passengers two-abreast with single aisle.
**Status:** Gulfstream I first flown, as long-range corporate transport, on 14 August 1958. G-1C conversion by Gulfstream American first flown on 25 October 1979.
**Sales:** Total of 200 Gulfstream I built. About 20 in airline service in 1987. Five G-1C conversions made.
**Notes:** The Gulfstream I was the first corporate transport produced by Grumman (followed in due course by the Gulfstream II twin jet). Total production was for the business market but the type was later adopted in small numbers as a regional airliner with 20–24 seats. Users in 1986 included Brown Air Services and Peregrine Air Services in the UK, and Royale Airlines in the US—the latter company using its Gulfstreams to feed the Continental Airlines 'hub' at Houston. After Gulfstream American had acquired rights in the Grumman commercial aircraft, the G-1C was developed, with the fuselage lengthened by 11 ft 7 in (3,53 m), and up to 37 seats three-abreast.

## GRUMMAN GULFSTREAM I

**Dimensions:** Span, 78 ft 6 in (23,92 m); length, 63 ft 9 in (19,43 m); height, 22 ft 9 in (6,94 m); wing area, 610.3 sq ft (56,7 m$^2$).
**Weights:** Operating weight empty, 21,900 lb (9 933 kg); max payload, 4,270 lb (1 937 kg); max take-off, 35,100 lb (15 920 kg); max landing, 33,600 lb (15 240 kg); max zero fuel, 26,170 lb (11 870 kg).

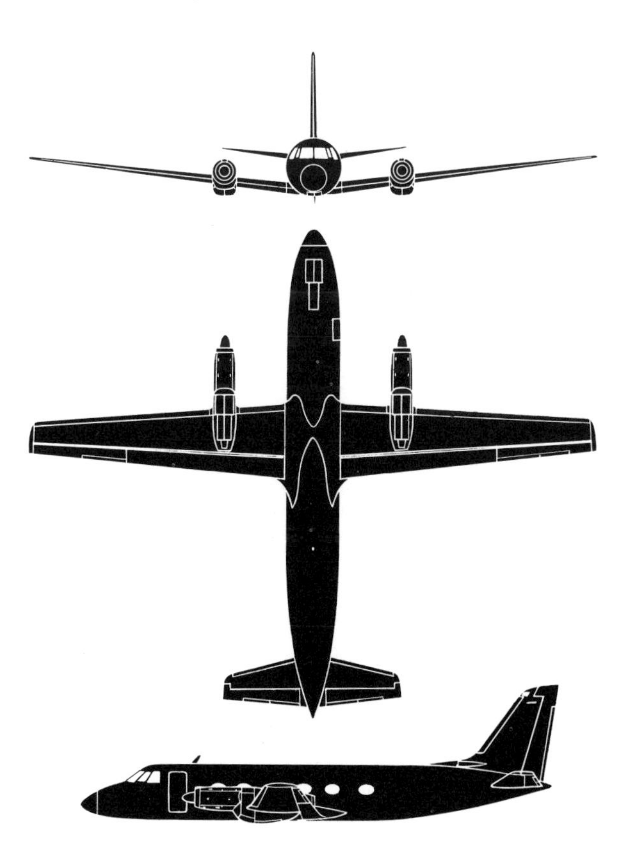

## GRUMMAN G-111

**Country of Origin:** USA.
**Type:** Light transport amphibian.
**Power Plant:** Two 1,475 hp (1 100 kW) Wright R-1820-982C9HE3 air-cooled piston radial engines.
**Performance:** Economical cruise, 162 kts (300 km/h) at 5,000 ft (1 525 m); range with max (28-passenger) payload, 273 naut mls (506 km) from land and 405 naut mls (750 km) from water.
**Accommodation:** Flight crew of two and up to 28 passengers, basically arranged in seats four-abreast with centre aisle at 32-in (81-cm) pitch.
**Status:** Prototype (military XJR2F-1) first flown 24 October 1947. First G-111 conversion flown 13 February 1979, certificated 29 April 1980, entered service (Chalk's International) July 1981.
**Sales:** More than 50 available for conversion: initial sales to Resort International (Chalks) and Pelita Air Services.
**Notes:** The G-111 amphibian is a civilianized HU-16 Albatross, the latter being a search-and-rescue and general utility aircraft built in large quantities for the USAF and US Navy. Grumman developed the conversion package for surplus HU-16s initially in co-operation with Resorts International which required such aircraft for use by its subsidiary Chalk's on scheduled services between Florida and Nassau. Up to 200 aircraft are available for conversion, of which Grumman had acquired 57 by end-1982 and had delivered five, with work on a second batch of seven under way. All 12 were delivered to Resorts International, which sold one to Pelita Air Service in Indonesia. Others are used by Chalk's. A turboprop version, with 1,645 shp Garrett TPE331-15 engines, has been projected and would have improved performance as well as a 2,000-lb (907-kg) increase in useful load.

## GRUMMAN G-111

**Dimensions:** Span, 96 ft 8 in (29,46 m); length, 61 ft 3 in (18,67 m); height, 25 ft 10 in (7,87 m); wing area, 1,035 sq ft (96,15 $m^2$).
**Weights:** Empty equipped, 23,500 lb (10 660 kg); max payload (cargo), over 8,000 lb (3 630 kg); max fuel, 6,438 lb (2 920 kg); max take-off, 30,800 lb (13 970 kg) from land, 31,150 lb (14 129 kg) from water; max landing, 29,160 lb (13 226 kg) on land, 31,150 lb (14 129 kg) on water.

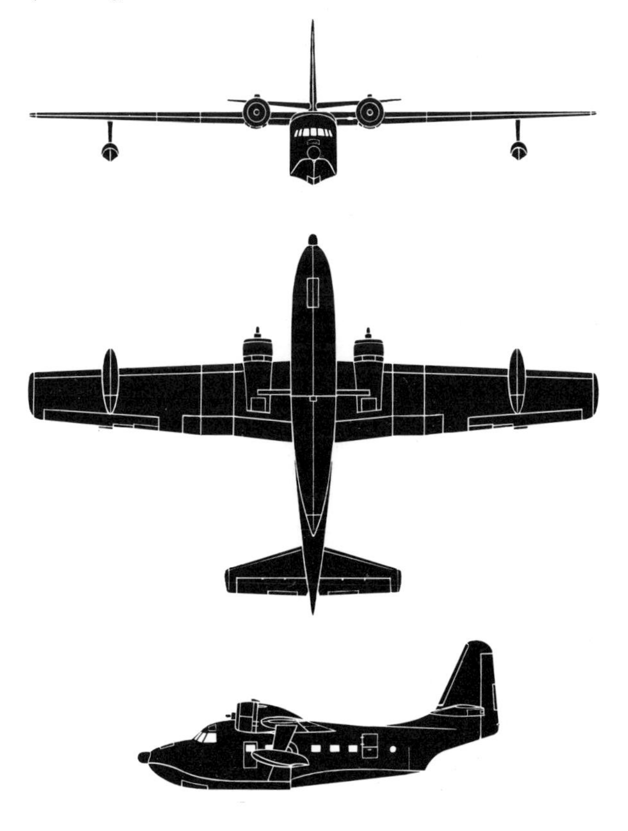

## HARBIN Y-12

**Country of Origin:** China.
**Type:** Light general purpose transport.
**Power Plant** (Y-12-II): Two 620 shp (462 kW) Pratt & Whitney PT6A-27 turboprops.
**Performance** (Y-12-II): Max cruising speed, 177 kts (328 km/h) at 9,840 ft (3 000 m); long-range cruising speed, 124 kts (230 km/h) at 9,840 ft (3 000 m); range with max payload, 135 naut mls (250 km); range with max fuel and a payload of 1,763 lb (800 kg), 777 naut mls (1 440 km).
**Accommodation:** Flight crew of two and up to 17 passengers three-abreast with offset aisle at 31.5-in (80-cm) pitch.
**Status:** Y-11 first flown in late 'seventies, certificated 1981. Y-21-I prototype flown 14 July 1982. Y-12-II certificated December 1985. In production in 1987.
**Sales:** In production for Chinese domestic use.
**Notes:** Development of a light general purpose twin-engined monoplane was started by the Harbin Aircraft Manufacturing Corporation in 1975, the aircraft being designated Y-11. A high wing monoplane of conventional design and construction, the seven-seat Y-11 was powered by 285 hp (213 kW) HS-6A piston engines and about 40 examples were built in the early 'eighties. Of similar configuration but extensively redesigned, the Y-12 appeared in 1982, featuring turboprop power, a new wing aerofoil and an enlarged fuselage. With PT6A-11 engines, this became the Y-12-I; the more powerful production version is designated Y-12-II. HAECO in Hong Kong has developed an avionics fit for the Y-12-II, using Western equipment.

## HARBIN Y-12-II

**Dimensions:** Span, 56 ft 6½ in (17,24 m); length, 48 ft 9 in (14,86 m); height, 18 ft 3 in (5,58 m); wing area, 368.9 sq ft (34,27 m²).
**Weights:** Operating weight empty, 6,614 lb (3 000 kg); max payload, 3,748 lb (1 700 kg); max fuel, 2,645 lb (1 200 kg); max take-off, 5,300 lb (11 684 kg); max landing, 11,023 lb (5 000 kg).

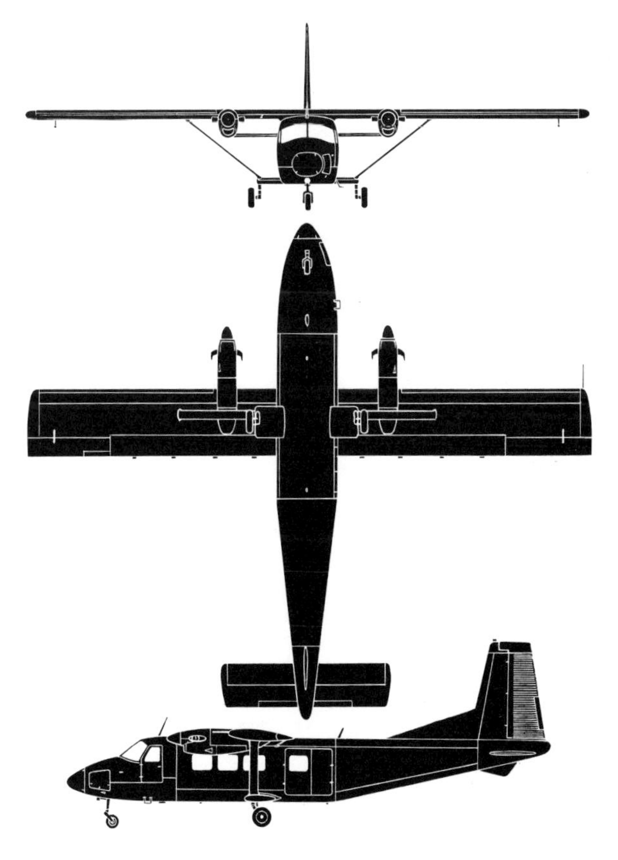

## ILYUSHIN IL-18

**Country of Origin:** Soviet Union.
**Type:** Medium-range turboprop airliner.
**Power Plant:** Four 4,250 ehp (3 169 kW) Ivchenko AI-20M turboprops.
**Performance:** Max cruising speed, 364 kts (675 km/h); economical cruising speed, 337 kts (625 km/h); range with max payload, 1,997 naut mls (3 700 km); range with max fuel, 3,508 naut mls (6 500 km).
**Accommodation:** Normal flight crew of five (two pilots, flight engineer, navigator and radio operator). Standard accommodation for 110 passengers in two cabins six-abreast and a rear compartment five-abreast. Max accommodation, 122.
**Status:** Prototype Il-18 first flown 4 July 1957; service use began (with Aeroflot) 20 April 1959. Production completed during 1968.
**Sales:** More than 600 Il-18s built, including approximately 100 exported to Communist Bloc countries in Europe, several African airlines, Cuba and China, and elsewhere.
**Notes:** A contemporary of the Antonov An-10, the Il-18 soon proved superior in the passenger-carrying rôle and in the two decades of the 'sixties and the 'seventies it played a major rôle in the expansion and modernisation of Aeroflot services within the Soviet Union and on international services in Europe and the Middle East. The 84-passenger Il-18V was the initial standard version, with 4,000 ehp (2 983 kW) AI-20K engines; the Il-18E had more power and a revised interior, and the Il-18D (data above) had increased fuel and a higher gross weight.

## ILYUSHIN IL-18D

**Dimensions:** Span, 122 ft 8½ in (37,40 m); length, 117 ft 9 in (35,9 m); height, 33 ft 4 in (10,17 m); wing area, 1,507 sq ft (140 m²).
**Weights:** Empty equipped, 77,160 lb (35 000 kg); max payload, 29,750 lb (13 500 kg); max take-off, 141,100 lb (64 000 kg).

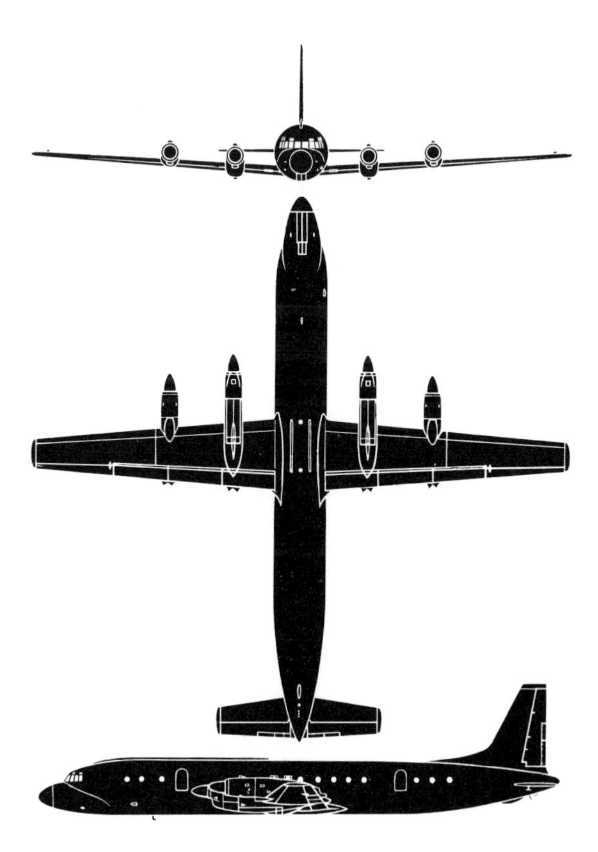

## ILYUSHIN IL-62

**Country of Origin:** Soviet Union.
**Type:** Long-range jet transport.
**Power Plant:** Four (Il-62) 23,150 lb st (10 500 kgp) Kuznetsov NK-8-4 or (Il-62M) 24,250 lb st (11 000 kgp) Soloviev D-30KU turbofans.
**Performance** (Il-62M): Typical cruising speed, 442–486 kts (820–900 km/h) at 35,000 ft (10 670 m); range with max payload, 4,210 naut mls (7 800 km); range with payload of 22,045 lb (10 000 kg), 5,400 naut mls (10 000 km).
**Accommodation:** Flight crew of five (two pilots, flight engineer, navigator and radio operator); maximum accommodation in two cabins for 186 passengers (174 in Il-62M, 195 in Il-62MK), six-abreast at a pitch of 34 in (86 cm) with central aisle.
**Sales:** Prototype first flown January 1963 (with Lyulka AL-7 engines); service introduction (with Aeroflot) 15 September 1967. Il-62M first flown 1971 and entered service 1974; Il-62MK introduced 1978.
**Sales:** Approximately 150 built for Aeroflot and 50 for export, including CSA (8 plus 4 Il-62M), Interflug (7 plus 8 Il-62M), LOT (6 plus 7 Il-62M), Tarom (4 plus 2 Il-62M), Cubana (10 Il-62M) and CAAC (5).
**Notes:** The Il-62 was the first Soviet jetliner designed for long-range intercontinental operations. The original production version was powered by Kuznetsov NK-8-4 turbofans but the improved Il-62M, appearing in 1971, has Soloviev D-30s of greater thrust and lower specific fuel consumption, combined with a fin fuel tank for longer range. The Il-62MK has a higher gross weight (368,170 lb/167 000 kg), increasing payload to 195 passengers.

## ILYUSHIN IL-62

**Dimensions:** Span, 141 ft 9 in (43,20 m); length, 174 ft 3½ in (53,12 m); height, 40 ft 6¼ in (12,35 m); wing area, 3,009 sq ft (279,55 m).

**Weights:** Operational weight empty, approximately 157,630 lb (71 500 kg); max payload, 50,700 lb (23 000 kg); max zero fuel, 208,550 lb (94 600 kg); max take-off, 363,760 lb (165 000 kg); max landing, 231,500 kg (105 000 kg).

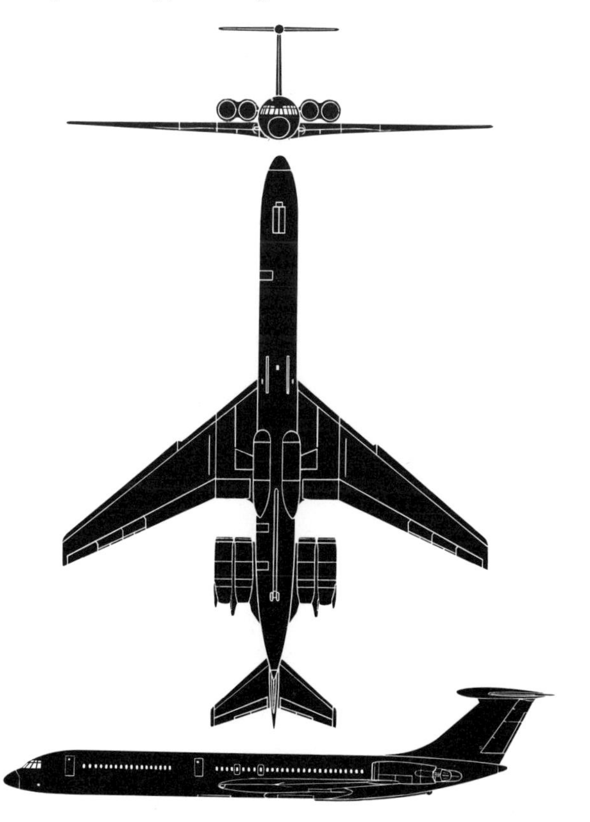

## ILYUSHIN IL-76

**Country of Origin:** Soviet Union.
**Type:** Long-range military and civil freighter.
**Power Plant:** Four 26,455 lb st (12 000 kgp) Soloviev D-30KP turbofans.
**Performance:** Max level speed, 459 kts (850 km/h); typical cruise, 405–432 kts (750–800 km/h); range with max payload, 2,700 naut mls (5 000 km); max range, 3,617 naut mls (6 700 km).
**Accommodation:** Normal flight crew of five (two pilots, flight engineer, navigator, radio operator) plus two freight handlers. Pressurized main cabin, with freight handling equipment, can accomodate one, two or three 30-passenger self-contained modules.
**Status:** Prototype first flown 25 March 1971. Service use by Aeroflot began 1975.
**Sales:** About 100 Il-76T and Il-76M in service with Aeroflot by end of 1986; exports to Iraqi Airways, Cubana, Jamahiriya of Libya, Syrianair and Bakhtar Afghan Airlines, totalling more than 50 (for military as well as civil use). More than 100 aircraft in service with Soviet Transport Aviation force.
**Notes:** Development of this long-range freighter was put in hand in the late 'sixties to provide a replacement for the turboprop An-12, with greater capabilities. Like the Antonov aircraft, the Il-76 has military as well as commercial applications, but those flown by Aeroflot are used primarily to carry heavy supplies associated with engineering and construction activities in the more remote areas of the Soviet Union. Early production aircraft were designated Il-76T; a version called the Il-76TD appeared subsequently and has improved D-30KP-1 engines, more fuel and higher operating weights. Il-76M and MD are military versions.

## ILYUSHIN IL-76T

**Dimensions:** Span, 165 ft 8 in (50,50 m); length, 152 ft $10\frac{1}{2}$ in (46,59 m); height, 48 ft 5 in (14,76 m); wing area, 3,229.2 sq ft (300 $m^2$).
**Weights:** Max payload, 88,185 lb (40 000 kg); max take-off weight, 374,785 lb (170 000 kg).

# ILYUSHIN IL-86

**Country of Origin:** Soviet Union.
**Type:** Long-range jetliner.
**Power Plant:** Four 28,660 lb st (13 000 kgp) Kuznetsov NK-86 turbofans.
**Performance:** Typical cruising speed, 485–512 kts (900–950 km/h) at 35,000 ft (10 670m); range with payload of 88,185 lb (40 000 kg), 1,945 naut mls (3 600 km); range with max fuel, 2,480 naut mls (4 600 km).
**Accommodation:** Normal flight crew of three (two pilots and flight engineer) plus provision for navigator. Maximum of 350 passengers, nine-abreast with two aisles; typical mixed class layout, 28 six-abreast in forward cabin and 206 eight-abreast in main and rear cabins.
**Status:** First of two prototypes flown at Moscow on 22 December 1976. First production-configured aircraft flown 24 October 1977. Proving flights began September 1978 and first scheduled service flown by Aeroflot 26 December 1980, and first international service (Moscow–East Berlin) 3 July 1981.
**Sales:** About 50 in service with Aeroflot in 1986. No exports.
**Notes:** The Il-86 is the Soviet Union's first 'airbus' type with a twin-aisle layout in the wide-body cabin; at first projected with a rear-engined layout, it was eventually built in the form illustrated after analysing the structural weight penalties and low-speed handling difficulties of the latter. Major Il-86 airframe components are produced in Poland, and final assembly takes place at Voronezh in the USSR. Up to the end of 1986, Aeroflot was the only operator of the type. A re-engined long-range variant of the design is designated Il-96 and is described separately on the following pages.

## ILYUSHIN IL-86

**Dimensions:** Span, 157 ft 8¼ in (48,06 m); length, 195 ft 4 in (59,54 m); height, 51 ft 10½ in (15,81 m); wing area, 3,444 sq ft (320 m²).

**Weights:** Max payload, 92,600 lb (42 000 kg); max fuel load, 189,600 lb (86 000 kg); max take-off, 454,150 lb (206 000 kg); max landing, 385,800 lb (175 000 kg).

## ILYUSHIN IL-96

**Country of Origin:** Soviet Union.
**Type:** Long-range large capacity jet transport.
**Power Plant:** Four 35,300 lb st (16 000 kgp) turbofans of unspecified type (believed to be Soloviev).
**Performance:** Max cruising speed, 486 kts (900 km/h) at 39,370 ft (12 000 m); best economy cruising speed, 459 kts (850 km/h); range with 66,150-lb (30 000-kg) payload, 4,860 naut mls (9 000 km); range with 33,070-lb (15 000-kg) payload, 5,940 naut mls (11 000 km); range with max payload, 4,050 naut mls (7 500 km).
**Accommodation:** Flight crew of three and up to 300 passengers, basically nine-abreast with two aisles; typical mixed-class layout for 22 first-class, 40-business class and 173 tourist-class at 41.5 to 34.3-in (102–77-cm) seat pitch.
**Status:** Under development for first flight in 1990.
**Sales:** None to date. Production for Aeroflot planned.
**Notes:** Derived from the Il-86 (see previous pages), the Il-96 is one of the types that Aeroflot plans to introduce during the 'nineties. Although of the same overall configuration as the Il-86, the Il-96 is extensively redesigned, having a wing of slightly greater span and area, but of reduced sweepback and with large winglets. The engines, not yet publicly identified, are believed to be of Soloviev design, and probably developed specially to give the best possible economy of operation in an aircraft of this type. A modern flight deck design has been adopted for the Il-96, with a six-display 'glass' cockpit for electronic presentation of information.

## ILYUSHIN IL-96

**Dimensions:** Span (excluding winglets), 189 ft 2 in (57,66 m); length, 181 ft 7 in (55,35 m); height, 57 ft $7\frac{3}{4}$ in (17,57 m); wing area, 3,767 sq ft (3 500 m$^2$).
**Weights:** Empty equipped, 257,940 lb (117 000 kg); max payload, 88,180 lb (40 000 kg); max take-off, 507,060 lb (230 000 kg).

## ILYUSHIN IL-114

**Country of Origin:** Soviet Union.
**Type:** Short-to-medium range regional turboprop transport.
**Power Plant:** Two 2,465 shp (1 840 kW) turboprops of unspecified type.
**Performance:** Max cruising speed, 270 kts (500 km/h) at 24,600 ft (7 500 m); range with 7,720-lb (3 500-kg) payload, 1,540 naut mls (2 850 km); range with 11,900-lb (5 400-kg) payload, 540 naut mls (1 000 km).
**Accommodation:** Flight crew of two and up to 60 passengers four-abreast with central aisle at 29.5-in (75-cm) pitch.
**Status:** Under development for testing in 1990.
**Sales:** None to date. Production for Aeroflot planned, for service introduction in the 'nineties.
**Notes:** The Il-114 has been designed as a successor for the Antonov An-24, to serve on Aeroflot routes with ranges of up to about 540 naut mls (1 000 km), and is one of a trio of types that were under development in the late 'eighties to provide for modernization of the Aeroflot fleet in the 'nineties. The Il-114—which is strikingly similar to the British Aerospace ATP, an aircraft in the same class—makes much use of composite materials and advanced metal alloys, including titanium, in its structure. Avionics and flight systems are of a standard to allow the Il-114 to operate in weather minima down to ICAO Cat II standard. The Polish aircraft industry is responsible for the propellers and the undercarriage.

## ILYUSHIN IL-114

**Dimensions:** Span, 98 ft 5 in (30,0 m); length, 83 ft $6\frac{1}{2}$ in (25,46 m); height, 28 ft $2\frac{1}{2}$ in (8,60 m); wing area, 796,6 sq ft (74 $m^2$).
**Weights:** Empty equipped, 28,660 lb (13 000 kg); max pay-load, 13,230 lb (6 000 kg); max take-off, 44,645 lb (22 250 kg).

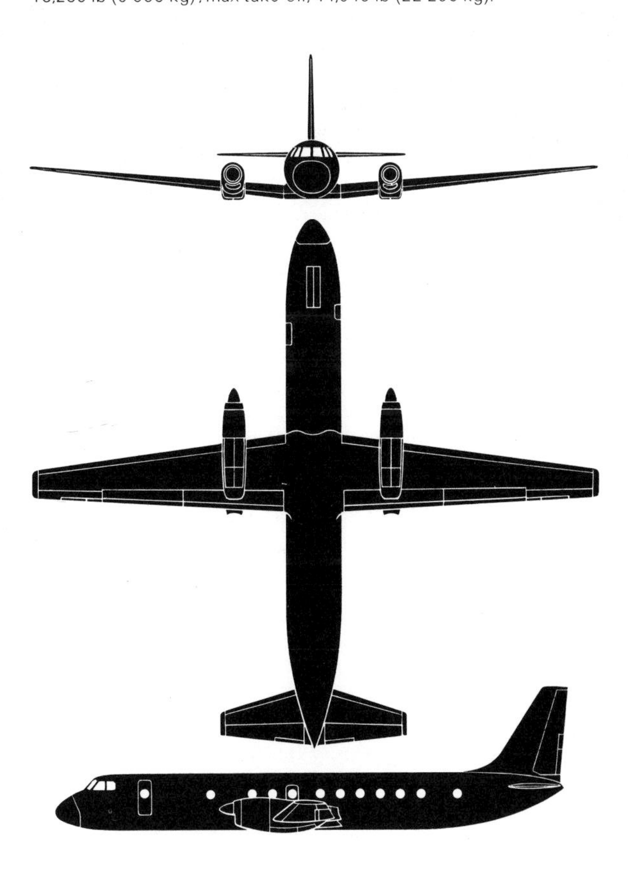

## LET L-410

**Country of Origin:** Czechoslovakia.
**Type:** Light turboprop transport.
**Power Plant:** Two 750 ehp (559 kW) Motorlet (Walter) M 601E turboprops.
**Performance:** Max cruise, 197 kts (365 km/h); economical cruise, 162 kts (300 km/h); range with max payload, 210 naut mls (390 km); range with max fuel, 561 naut mls (1 040 km).
**Accommodation:** Flight crew of two and 15 passengers three-abreast with off-set aisle at 30-in (76-cm) pitch.
**Status:** Prototype L-410 flown on 16 April 1969. First L-410M flown 1973. Prototype L-410 UVP flown 1 November 1977, certificated and entered service 1980. L-410 UVP-E first flown late 1984.
**Sales:** Primary customer is Aeroflot, which took delivery of its 500th L-410 in March 1985, with deliveries continuing.
**Notes:** Development of the L-410 light transport began at the Kunovice works of the Let National Corporation (Let Národni Podnik) in 1966, as the first complete aircraft project undertaken by that factory. The first 31 aircraft were completed as L-410As with Pratt & Whitney PT6A-27 engines and saw some service with CSA and Slov-Air, as did the L-410M with M-601 engines (110 built). The L-410 UVP is the definitive production version, adopted by Aeroflot for use on regional services; this has a slightly longer fuselage, dihedral on the tailplane and numerous other improvements. The L-410 has five-bladed propellers, tip tanks and more powerful engines. A larger transport of similar configuration, the LET L-610, was under development in 1987 and was expected to fly in 1988. To be certificated in 1990, the L-610 will seat up to 40 passengers and will be powered by 1,822 shp Motorlet M 602 turboprops.

## LET L-410 UVP

**Dimensions:** Span, 63 ft 10$\frac{3}{4}$ in (19,48 m); length, 47 ft 5$\frac{1}{2}$ in (14,47 m); height, 19 ft 1$\frac{1}{2}$ in (5,83 m); wing area, 378.67 sq ft (35,18 $m^2$).
**Weights:** Empty equipped, 8,378 lb (3 800 kg); max payload, 2,888 lb (1 310 kg); max fuel, 2,205 lb (1 000 kg); max zero fuel, 11,398 lb (5 170 kg); max take-off, 12,786 lb (5 800 kg); max landing, 12,125 lb (5 500 kg).

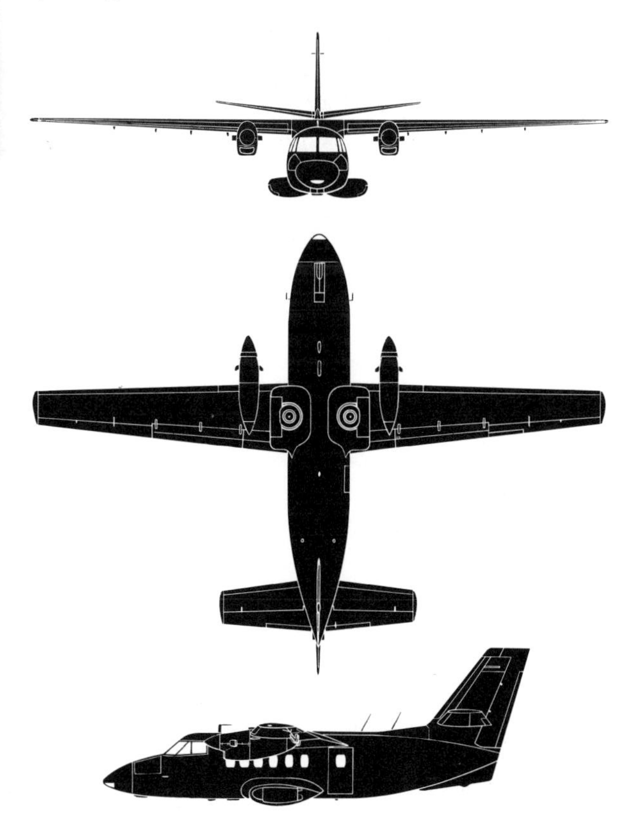

## LOCKHEED ELECTRA

**Country of Origin:** USA.
**Type:** Short-medium range passenger and cargo transport.
**Power Plant:** Four 3,750 ehp (2 800 kW) Allison 501-D13 turboprops.
**Performance:** Max cruise, 352 kts (652 km/h) at 22,000 ft (6 700 m); best economy cruise, 325 kts (602 km/h); range with max payload, 1,910 naut mls (3 540 km); range with max fuel, 2,180 naut mls (4 023 km).
**Accommodation:** Flight crew of two or three, and up to 98 passengers six-abreast at 38-in (96.5-cm) pitch; typical mixed-class layout for 16 first class and 51 tourist class.
**Status:** First of four development aircraft flown 6 December 1957, first production-standard aircraft flown 19 May 1958. Certification 22 August 1958, entered service (Eastern Airlines) 12 January 1959. Re-certification of modified aircraft 5 January 1961. Production completed.
**Sales:** Total production 170 including 55 L-188C version.
**Notes:** Electra was first airliner of US design and production with turbine power to enter commercial service, and proved to be the only large airliner of US origin to use turboprops. Basic variant was L-188A, and L-188C had extra fuel and was certificated for higher weights, being intended primarily for overwater operations. About half of all Electras built remain in service, the majority of these having been converted for use as freighters, with large loading doors in the rear fuselage side and strengthened cabin flooring incorporating roller conveyors to facilitate the handling of pallets and containers. These conversions were made by such companies as Lockheed Aircraft Service and American Jet Industries.

## LOCKHEED ELECTRA L-188A

**Dimensions:** Span, 99 ft 0 in (30,18 m); length, 104 ft 6 in (31,81 m); height, 32 ft 10 in (10,0 m); wing area, 1,300 sq ft (120,8 m²).
**Weights:** Empty equipped, 61,500 lb (27 895 kg); max payload, 26,500 lb (12 020 kg); max fuel, 37,500 lb (17 010 kg); max zero fuel, 86,000 lb (39 010 kg); max take-off, 116,000 lb (52 664 kg); max landing, 95,650 lb (43 387 kg).

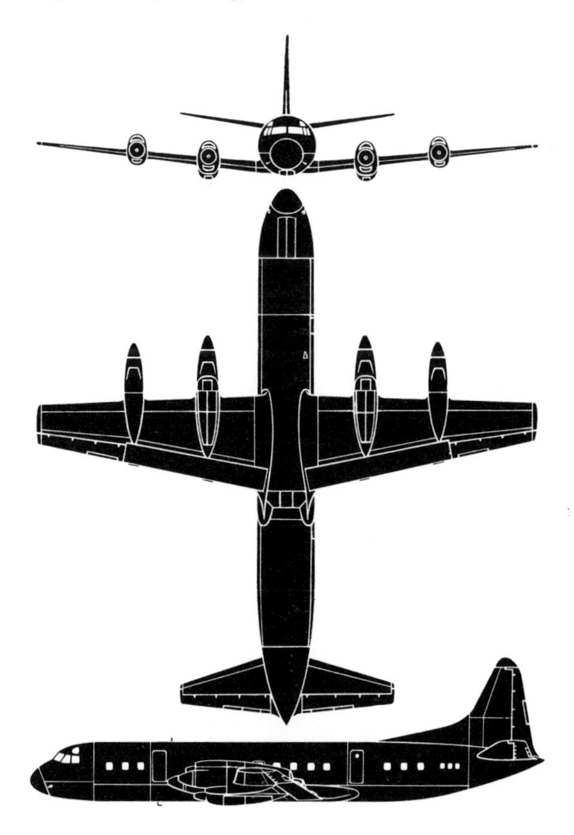

## LOCKHEED L-100 HERCULES

**Country of Origin:** USA.
**Type:** Turboprop cargo transport.
**Power Plant:** Four, 4,680 ehp (3 490 kW) Allison 501-D22A turboprops.
**Performance:** Max cruise, 315 kts (583 km/h) at 20,000 ft (6 100 m); long-range cruise, 300 kts (556 km/h); range with max payload (-20), 2,100 naut mls (3 889 km); (-30), 1,363 naut mls (2 526 km); range with max fuel (zero payload) (-20), 4,250 naut mls (7 871 km), (-30), 4,980 naut mls (9 227 km).
**Accommodation:** Flight crew of three or four; usually all-freight configuration; provision for up to 91 passengers accommodated in quick-fit modules.
**Status:** Lockheed Model 382-44K-20 civil Hercules first flown 21 April 1964 and certificated 16 February 1965. L-100-20 first flown 19 April 1968, certificated 4 October 1968, L-100-30 first flown 14 August 1970, certificated 7 October 1970.
**Sales:** More than 100 L-100 commercial Hercules by 1986, within overall Hercules production of more than 1,800.
**Notes:** The L-100 designation applies to commercial models of the C-130 Hercules, although a few early examples were known by the Lockheed Model 382B designation. The early L-100s were dimensionally similar to the C-130, but the L-100-20 has the fuselage stretched by 8 ft 4 in (2,54 m) and the L-100-30 is longer by another 20 ft (6,1 m). A few L-100s have been bought as high-density low-cost passenger transports and Lockheed has projected a dedicated passenger-carrying version as well as further stretches, such as the L-100-50 with a total fuselage stretch of 36 ft 8 in (11,18 m) and higher gross weight.

## LOCKHEED L-100-30

**Dimensions:** Span, 132 ft 7 in (40,41 m); length, 112 ft 9 in (34,37 m); height, 38 ft 3 in (11,66 m); wing area, 1,745 sq ft (162,12 m²).
**Weights:** Operating empty, 77,680 lb (35 235 kg); max payload, 51,110 lb (23 183 kg); max fuel weight, 64,856 lb (29,418 kg); max take-off, 155,000 lb (70 308 kg); max landing, 135,000 lb (61 236 kg).

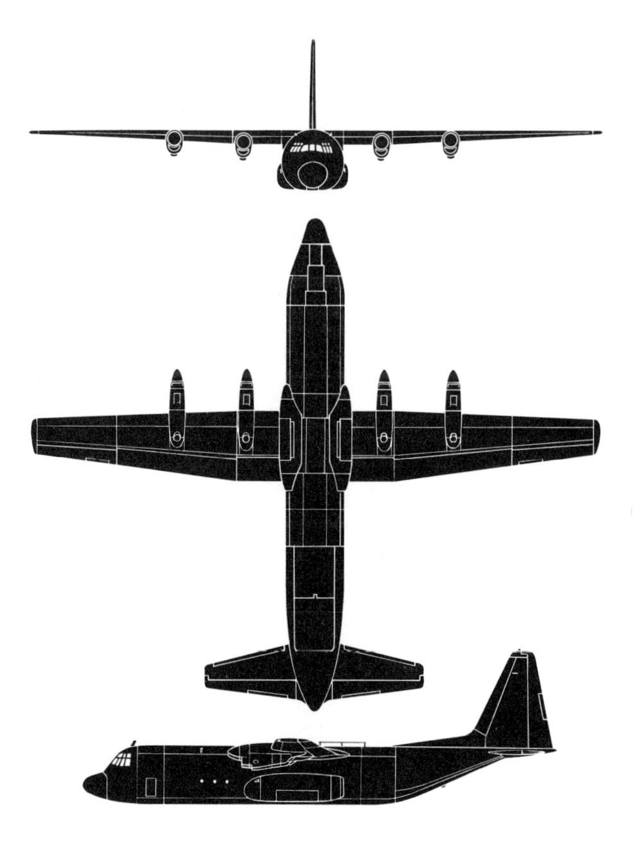

# LOCKHEED L-1011-100, -200 TRISTAR

**Country of Origin:** USA.
**Type:** Medium/long-range large-capacity airliner.
**Power Plant:** Three (-1, -100) 42,000 lb st (19 050 kgp) Rolls-Royce RB.211-22B or (-200) 50,000 lb st (22 680 kgp) RB.211-524 turbofans.
**Performance** (L-1011-200): Max cruising speed at mid-cruise weight, 526 kts (973 km/h) at 30,000 ft (9 145 m); economical cruising speed, 463 kts (890 km/h) at 35,000 ft (10 670 m); range with max passenger payload, 5,812 naut mls (6 690 km); range with max fuel, 4,918 naut mls (9 111 km).
**Accommodation:** Flight crew of three and up to 400 passengers 10-abreast with two aisles, at 30-in (76-cm) seat pitch; typical mixed-class, 256, basically nine-abreast.
**Status:** First L-1011 flown 17 November 1970 and fifth, completing the development batch, on 2 December 1971. Provisional certification 22 December 1971; full certification 14 April 1972 and first service (Eastern) 30 April. First flight with RB.211-524 engines, 12 August 1976, certification of -200 on 26 April 1977 and entered service with Saudia. Production completed 1984.
**Sales:** Total of 249 built for 16 airlines (including L-1011-500, see next entry), plus one company-owned prototype. Eighteen airlines operating -1, -100, and -200 models in 1987.
**Notes:** Lockheed launched the Tristar in March 1968 as the second of the wide-body transports. The -100 differs from the original -1 in having higher weights and more fuel, while the -200 is like the -100 but with uprated engines. The -250 is a -1 conversion with RB.211-524B4 engines.

## LOCKHEED L-1011-200 TRISTAR

**Dimensions:** Span, 155 ft 4 in (47,34 m); length, 177 ft 8½ in (54,17 m); height, 55 ft 4 in (16,87 m); wing area, 3,456 sq ft (320,0 m²).
**Weights:** Operating weight empty, 248,000 lb (112 670 kg); max payload, 89,600 lb (40 642 kg); max fuel weight, 176,930 lb (80 254 kg); max zero fuel, 338,000 lb (153 315 kg); max take-off, 466,000 lb (211 375 kg); max landing, 368,000 lb (166 920 kg).

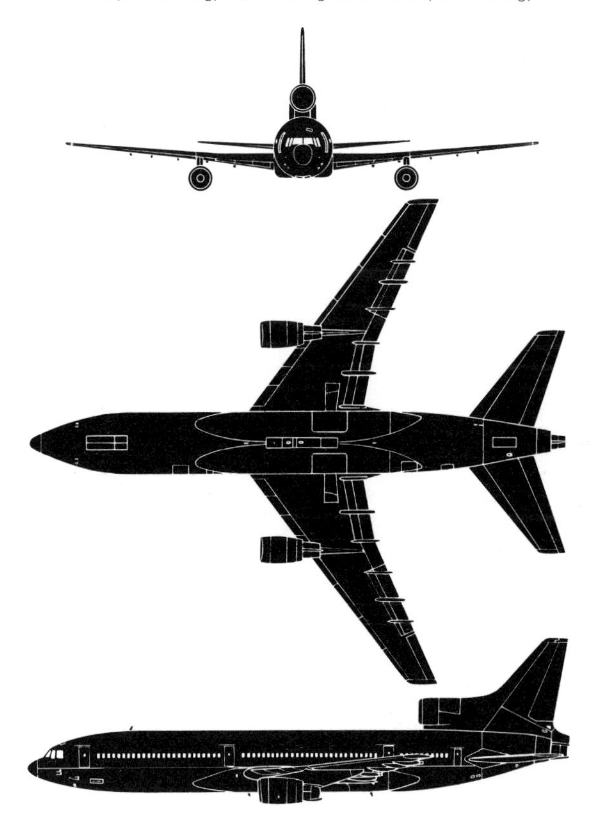

## LOCKHEED L-1011-500 TRISTAR

**Country of Origin:** USA.
**Type:** Long-range large-capacity airliner.
**Power Plant:** Three 50,000 lb st (22 680 kgp) Rolls-Royce RB.211-524B or B4 turbofans.
**Performance:** Max cruising speed at mid-cruise weight, 518 kts (959 km/h) at 33,000 ft (10 000 m); economical cruising speed, 483 kts (894 km/h) at 35,000 ft (10 670 m); range with max passenger payload, 5,345 naut mls (9 905 km); range with max fuel, 6,100 naut mls (11 260 km).
**Accommodation:** Flight crew of three and up to 330 passengers 10-abreast with two aisles at 30/33-in (76/83-cm) pitch; typical mixed class, 24F (six-abreast) and 222T (nine-abreast).
**Status:** First L-1011-500 flown 16 October 1978; extended wing-tips first flown (on original L-1011-1 prototype) in 1978 and on production -500 (with active ailerons) in November 1979. Entered service (British Airways, without active controls) 7 May 1979 and (Pan American, with active controls) early 1980. Certificated with fully-digital flight control system for Cat IIIA operations, 17 June 1981. Production completed 1984.
**Sales:** Ordered and/or operated by Aero Peru, Air Canada, Air Lanka, Alia, BWIA, Delta, LTU, Pan American and TAP (Air Portugal). British Airways fleet of six sold to RAF in 1983.
**Notes:** The TriStar 500 was launched in August 1976 as a derivative of the -200 (see previous page), to provide a transport of longer range and reduced capacity. It features active controls to reduce wing bending moments, an improved wing-to-fuselage fairing and an advanced flight management system. Wing span is increased and fuselage length reduced.

## LOCKHEED L-1011-500 TRISTAR

**Dimensions:** Span, 164 ft 4 in (50,09 m); length, 164 ft 2½ in (50,05 m); height, 55 ft 4 in (16,87 m); wing area, 3,540 sq ft (329,0 m²).
**Weights:** Operating weight empty, 245,400 lb (111 311 kg); max payload, 92,608 lb (42 006 kg); max fuel weight, 211,249 lb (95 821 kg); max zero fuel, 338,000 lb (153 315 kg); max take-off, 510,000 lb (231 330 kg); max landing, 368,000 lb (166 920 kg).

## McDONNELL DOUGLAS DC-8

**Country of Origin:** USA.
**Type:** Long-range medium capacity turbofan transport.
**Power Plant:** Four 22,000 lb st (9 980 kgp) CFM International CFM56-2-C5 turbofans.
**Performance** (Srs 73): Max cruising speed, 479 kts (887 km/h) at 39,000 ft (11 890 m); best economy cruising speed, 459 kts (850 km/h) at 39,000 ft (11 890 m); range with max payload, 4,830 naut mls (8 950 km).
**Accommodation** (Srs 73): Flight crew of three and up to 269 passengers six-abreast with central aisle at 30-in (76-cm) pitch.
**Status:** First flights: Srs 10, 30 May 1958; Srs 20, 29 November 1958; Srs 30, 21 February 1959; Srs 40, 23 July 1959; Srs 50, 20 December 1960; Srs 55 Jet Trader, 20 October 1962; Srs 61, 14 March 1966; Srs 62, 29 August 1966; Srs 63, 10 April 1967; Srs 71, 15 August 1981; Srs 72, 5 December 1981; Srs 73, 4 March 1982. Entry into service: Srs 10 (Delta, United) 18 September 1959; Srs 30 (Pan American) April 1960; Srs 40 (TCA) April 1960; Srs 61, 25 February 1967; Srs 62, 22 May 1967; Srs 63, 27 July 1967; Srs 71, 24 April 1982. Production completed, May 1972.
**Sales:** One prototype (unsold) and 555 DC-8s built, comprising 28 Srs 10, 24 Srs 20, 57 Srs 30, 32 Srs 40, 87 Srs 50, 54 Srs 55, 88 Srs 61, 68 Srs 62 and 107 Srs 63. 110 Sixty-series converted to Srs 70 versions.
**Notes:** Srs 10 to 50 were dimensionally similar to each other, with varying power plants, fuel capacity and weight; Srs 55 Jet Trader had cargo door. Srs 61 and 63 had 36 ft 8 in (11,18-m) fuselage stretch and Srs 62 had 6 ft 8 in (2,03 m) stretch. Srs 71, 72, 73 are conversions of 60-series with CFM56 engines.

## McDONNELL DOUGLAS DC-8 SRS 73

**Dimensions:** Span, 148 ft 5 in (45,20 m); length, 187 ft 5 in (57,1 m); height, 43 ft 0 in (13,1 m); wing area, 2,927 sq ft (271,9 m$^2$).
**Weights:** Operating weight empty, 166,500 lb (75 500 kg), max payload, 64,500 lb (29 257 kg); max fuel, 162,642 lb (73 773 kg); max take-off, 355,000 lb (161 025 kg); max landing, 258,000 lb (117 000 kg).

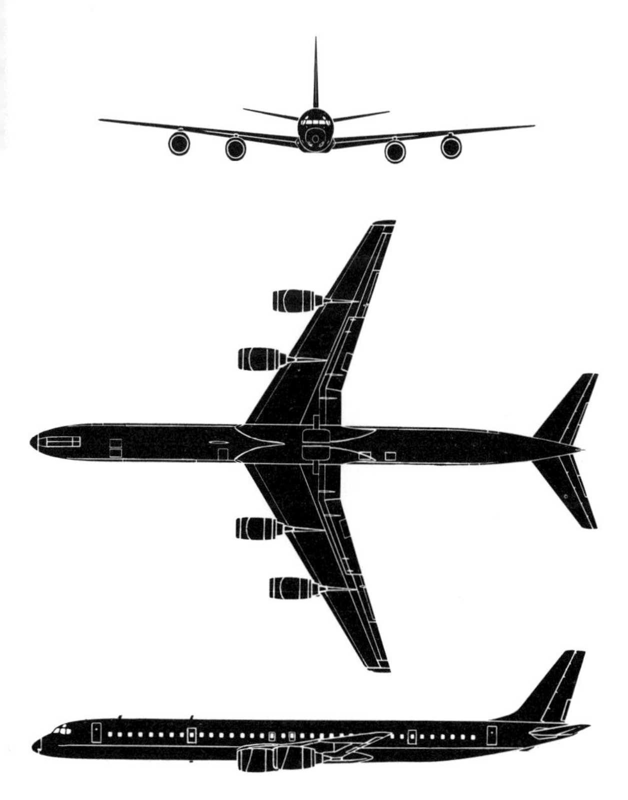

## McDONNELL DOUGLAS DC-9

**Country of Origin:** USA.
**Type:** Short-to-medium-range jet transport.
**Power Plant** (Srs 50): Two 15,000 lb st (7 030 kgp) Pratt & Whitney JT8D-15 or 16,000 lb st (7 257 kgp) JT8D-17 turbofans.
**Performance** (Srs 50): Max cruising speed, 501 kts (929 km/h) at 27,000 ft (8 230 m); long-range cruising speed, 440 kts (817 km/h) at 35,000 ft (10 670 m); range with 97-passenger payload, 1,796 naut mls (3 326 km).
**Accommodation:** Flight crew of two and up to 139 passengers five-abreast with offset aisle at 31-in (79-cm) pitch.
**Status:** First (Srs 10) development aircraft flown 25 February 1965; first Srs 30 flown 1 August 1966; first Srs 20 flown 18 September 1968. DC-9RF development aircraft (JT8D-109 engines) flown 9 January 1975. Certification: (Srs 10), 23 November 1965; (Srs 20), 11 December 1968; (Srs 30), 19 December 1966. Entry into service: Srs 10 (Delta), 8 December 1965; Srs 20 (SAS), 23 January 1969; Srs 30 (Eastern), 1 February 1967, Srs 40 first flown on 28 November 1967, certificated 27 February 1968, entered service (SAS) 12 March 1968. Srs 50 first flown 17 December 1974, entered service (Swissair) 24 August 1975.
**Sales:** Total of 976 DC-9s built, comprising 137 Srs 10, 10 Srs 20, 662 Srs 30 (including 43 military), 40 Srs 71 and 96 Srs 50. Series 80 redesignated MD-80—see next pages.
**Notes:** The most-produced DC-9 Srs 30 is 14 ft 11 in (4,6 m) longer than the Srs 10 and 20. Convertible (DC-9C) and freighter (DC-9F) versions were also produced. The Srs 40 and Srs 50 were successive stages of fuselage 'stretch'.

## McDONNELL DOUGLAS DC-9 SRS 50

**Dimensions:** Span, 93 ft 5 in (28,47 m); length, 119 ft $3\frac{1}{2}$ in (36,37 m); height, 27 ft 6 in (8,38 m); wing area, 1,000.7 sq ft (92,97 m$^2$).
**Weights:** Operating weight empty, 57,190 lb (25 940 kg); max payload, 31,000 lb (14 060 kg); max take-off 121,000 lb (54 885 kg); max landing, 110,000 lb (49 895 kg).

## McDONNELL DOUGLAS MD-80

**Country of Origin:** USA.
**Type:** Short/medium-range jet transport.
**Power Plant:** Two (MD-81) 18,500 lb st (8 390 kgp) Pratt & Whitney JT8D-209 turbofans with 750-lb st (340-kgp) reserve.
**Performance:** Max cruise, 499 kts (924 km/h) at 27,000 ft (8 230 m); long-range cruise, 439 kts (813 km/h) at 35,000 ft (10 670 m); range with 155-passenger payload (MD-81) 1,563 naut mls (2 896 km), (MD-82) 2,040 naut mls (3 778 km).
**Accommodation:** Flight crew of two and up to 172 passengers five-abreast, with off-set aisle, at 31-in (78-cm) seat pitch.
**Status:** Three development MD-80s first flown on 18 October 1979, 6 December 1979 and 29 February 1980; first MD-82 flown 8 January 1981; first MD-83 flown 17 December 1984. MD-81 certification on 26 August 1980; entry into service (Swissair) 5 October 1980. MD-82 certification 30 July 1981, entry into service (Republic) August 1982. MD-83 certificated November 1985 and first delivery to Finnair.
**Sales:** Total of 555 MD-80s sold by early 1987 (including MD-87—see next pages).
**Notes:** The MD-80 was launched as the DC-9 Super 80 in October 1977, as a 'stretched' Srs 50. The MD-81 and MD-82 differ in engine power and operating weights; also certificated is an MD-82 version with JT8D-217A engines and 149,500-lb (67 812-kg) gross weight. The MD-83 has a weight of 160,000 lb (72 576 kg) and greater range, with 21,000 lb st (9 526 kgp) JT8D-219 engines. MD-88 is as MD-82 with advanced avionics.

## McDONNELL DOUGLAS MD-81

**Dimensions:** Span, 107 ft 10 in (32,87 m); length, 147 ft 10 in (45,06 m); height, 29 ft 8 in (9,03 m); wing area, 1,270 sq ft (118 m²).
**Weights:** Operating empty, 78,420 lb (35 570 kg); max payload, 39,579 lb (17 952 kg); max fuel, 39,128 lb (17 748 kg); max zero fuel, 118,000 lb (53 524 kg); max take-off, 140,000 lb (63 500 kg); max landing, 128,000 lb (58 060 kg).

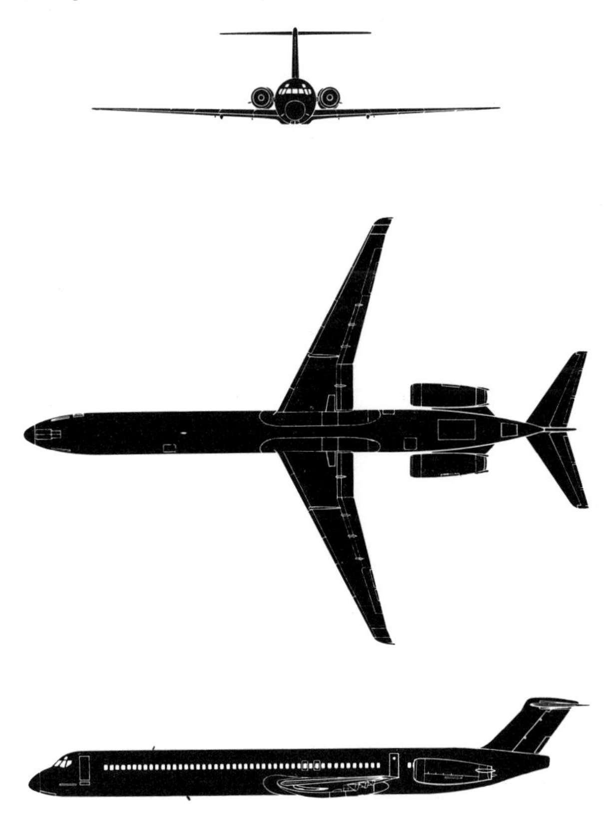

## McDONNELL DOUGLAS MD-87

**Country of Origin:** USA.
**Type:** Short-to-medium range jet transport.
**Power Plant:** Two 20,000 lb st (9 072 kgp) Pratt & Whitney JT8D-217C turbofans with 850-lb (836-kgp) thrust reserve.
**Performance:** Long-range cruising speed, 438 kts (811 km/h) at 35,000 ft (10 670 m); range with 130-passenger payload, 2,370 naut mls (4 395 km); range with auxiliary fuel, 2,833 naut mls (5 246 km).
**Accommodation:** Flight crew of two and up to 130 passengers five-abreast with offset aisle at 32-in (81-cm) pitch.
**Status:** Launch decision announced 3 January 1985 following purchase decision by Finnair and Austrian taken in December 1984. First prototype flown 4 December 1986. Certification and entry into service, late 1987.
**Sales:** Total of 32 firm sales by early 1987, for Finnair (8), Austrian Airlines (4), Toa Domestic (4), SAS (10), Aero Lloyd (2) and CTA Geneva (4).
**Notes:** The MD-87 was developed in the mid-eighties to combine the advanced features of the MD-80 series (see previous pages) with the shorter fuselage of the original DC-9 Srs 30, in order to provide an economic twin jet of smaller capacity than the earlier 155-seat MD-80s. The fuselage of the MD-87 is 17 ft 5 in (5,3 m) shorter than that of the basic MD-80 series, providing for a typical mixed-class layout with 117 seats. A small upward extension of the fin above the tailplane compensates for the shorter moment arm, but in all other respects the MD-87 is externally identical with its long-fuselage forerunners.

## McDONNELL DOUGLAS MD-87

**Dimensions:** Span, 107 ft 9½ in (32,86 m); length, 130 ft 5 in (39,7 m); height, 30 ft 6 in (9,29 m); wing area, 1,209 sq ft (112.0 $m^2$).
**Weights:** Operating weight empty, 73,274 lb (33 237 kg); max payload, 30,820 lb (13 980 kg); max fuel, 39,130 lb (17 750 kg); max take-off, 140,000 lb (63 503 kg); opt max take-off, 149,500 lb (67 813 kg); max landing, 128,000 lb (58 060 kg).

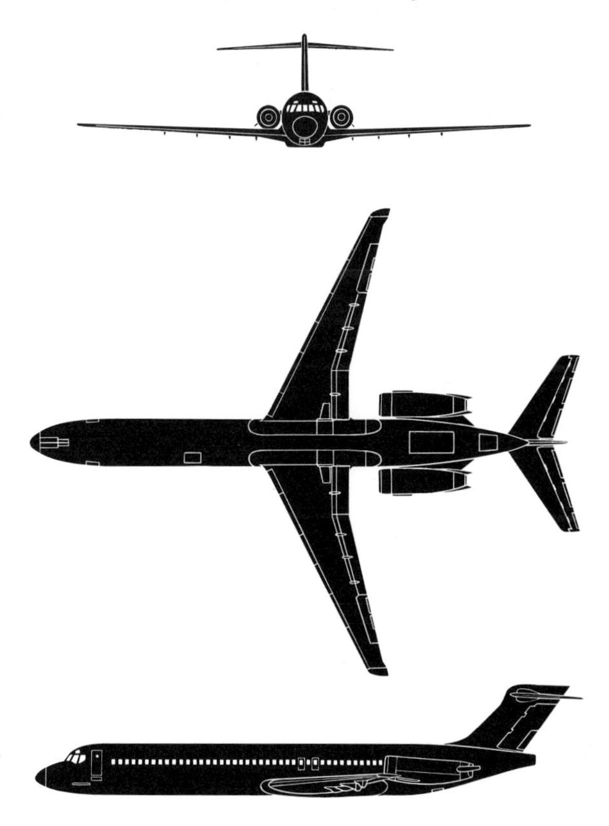

## McDONNELL DOUGLAS DC-10

**Country of Origin:** USA.
**Type:** Medium/long-range large-capacity airliner.
**Power Plant:** Three (Srs 30) 49,000 lb st (22 226 kgp) General Electric CF6-50A or 51,000 lb st (23 134 kgp) CF6-50C or 52,500 lb st (23 814 kgp) CF6-50C1 or C2 turbofans or (Srs 40) 49,400 lb st (22 408 kgp) Pratt & Whitney JT9D-20 or 53,000 lb st (24 040 kgp) JT9D-59A turbofans.
**Performance** (Srs 30): Max cruise, 490 kts (908 km/h) at 30,000 ft (9 154 m); long-range cruise, 475 kts (880 km/h) at 31,000 ft (9 450 m); range with max payload, 4,000 naut mls (7 413 km); ferry range with max fuel, (zero payload) 6,504 naut mls (12 055 km).
**Accommodation:** Flight crew of three and up to 380 passengers ten-abreast with two aisles at 32-in (81-cm) seat pitch.
**Status:** First three development DC-10s (Srs 10s) flown 29 August, 24 October and 23 December 1970; certificated 29 July 1971, entered service (American Airlines) 5 August 1971, Srs 15 first flown 8 January 1981, certificated 12 June 1981, entered service with Aeromexico, Srs 30 first flown 21 June 1972, certificated 21 November 1972, entered service with KLM and Swissair Srs 30CF flown 28 February 1973, first deliveries (to TIA and ONO) April 1973. Srs 40 first flown 28 February 1972, certificated 20 October 1972, entered service with Northwest Orient.
**Sales:** Total of 382 commercial DC-10s sold to end of 1986, plus 60 KC-10A military tankers.
**Notes:** The DC-10s is the third Douglas jetliner. Srs 10 was US domestic version and Srs 30 is principal intercontinental version, the Srs 40 being similar with switch from CF6 to JT9D engines. Production ends in 1988, in favour of MD-11.

## McDONNELL DOUGLAS DC-10 SRS 30

**Dimensions:** Span, 165 ft 4 in (50,40 m); length, 182 ft 1 in (55,50 m); height, 58 ft 1 in (17,7 m); wing area, 3,958 sq ft (367,7 m²).
**Weights:** Operating empty, 267,197 lb (121 198 kgp); max payload, 106,550 lb (48 330 kg); max fuel, 245,566 lb (111 387 kg); max zero fuel, 368,000 lb (166 922 kg); max take-off, 572,000 lb (259 450 kg); max landing, 403,000 lb (182 798 kg).

## McDONNELL DOUGLAS MD-11

**Country of Origin:** USA.
**Type:** Long-range large-capacity transport.
**Power Plant:** Three advanced-technology turbofans of 58,000–60,000 lb st (26 310–27 215 kgp) each, such as Pratt & Whitney PW 4358, General Electric CF6-80C2 or Rolls-Royce RB.211-535D4D.
**Performance:** Max cruising speed, 511 kts (946 km/h) at 31,000 ft (9 450 m); long-range cruising speed, 560 kts (898 km/h) at 31,000 ft (9 450 m); range with max payload, no reserves, 5,010 naut mls (9 260 km).
**Accommodation:** Flight crew of two and up to 405 passengers 10-abreast with two aisles, at 34/32-in (86/81-cm) pitch; typical mixed-class layout for 34 passengers six-abreast at 42/41-in (107/104-cm) pitch and 287 nine-abreast at 34/32-in (86/81-cm) pitch.
**Status:** First of two development MD-11s to fly March 1989. Certification, March 1990.
**Sales:** Twelve customers placed orders for total of 52 MD-11s, with options on 40 more, during December 1986 leading to year-end launch decision. Customers include British Caledonian, SAS, Swissair, Dragonair, Alitalia, Varig, Thai Airways, Korean Air and Federal Express.
**Notes:** The MD-11 emerged in 1984 as the latest of a number of projected derivative or stretched versions of the DC-10, and was finally launched at the end of 1986. The aircraft features an 18 ft 7 in (5,66 m) stretch of the DC-10 Srs 30 fuselage, together with a 10-ft (3,05-m) increase in wing span, combined with the addition of winglets. Other important innovations are a smaller tailplane containing fuel, usable for trim purposes; carbon brakes, advanced materials, a more flexible cabin interior and an advanced two-man flight deck with a digital Flight Management System.

## McDONNELL DOUGLAS MD-11

**Dimensions:** Span, 169 ft 6 in (51,70 m); length, 198 ft 7 in (60,50 m); height, 57 ft 9 in (17,60 m); wing area, 3,674 sq ft (341,3 m²).
**Weights:** Operating weight empty, 277,000 lb (125 646 kg); max payload, 123,000 lb (55 792 kg); max fuel, 260,000 lb (117 936 kg); max take-off, 602,500 lb (273 300 kg); max landing, 430,000 lb (195 047 kg).

# NAMC YS-11

**Country of Origin:** Japan.
**Type:** Short-range turboprop transport.
**Power Plant:** Two 3,060 shp (2 282 kW) Rolls-Royce Dart 542-10K turboprops.
**Performance:** Max cruising speed, 253 kts (469 km/h) at 15,000 ft (4 575 m); best economy cruise, 244 kts (452 km/h) at 20,000 ft (6 100 m); range with max payload (no reserves), 590 naut mls (1 090 km); range with max fuel (no reserves), 1,736 naut mls (3 215 km).
**Accommodation:** Flight crew of two or three and 60 passengers four-abreast with central aisle at 34-in (86-cm) pitch.
**Status:** Two prototypes flown on 30 August and 28 December 1962 respectively; first production YS-11 flown 23 October 1964, certification 25 August 1964, entered service (Toa Airways) April 1965. First YS-11A-200 flown 27 November 1967, certificated (by FAA) 3 April 1968. YS-11A-400 flown 17 September 1969. Production completed February 1974.
**Sales:** Production of the YS-11 totalled 182 (including prototypes), comprising 49 Srs 100, 95 Srs 200, 16 Srs 300, nine Srs 400, four Srs 500 and nine Srs 600; of the total, 23 sold initially to Japanese armed forces and remainder commercial. Over 100 in commercial service early 1987.
**Notes:** The YS-11 was Japan's first post-war commercial transport to enter production, having been designed and built by a consortium made up of Mitsubishi, Kawasaki, Fuji, Shin Meiwa, Japan Aircraft Manufacturing and Showa. The major users in 1987 were the Japanese domestic airlines TDA and All Nippon, and Mid Pacific Airlines in Hawaii.

## NAMC YS-11A-200

**Dimensions:** Span, 104 ft 11¾ in (32,00 m); length 86 ft 3½ in (26,30 m); height, 29 ft 5½ in (8,98 m); wing area, 1,020.4 sq ft (94,8 $m^2$).
**Weights:** Operating empty, 33,993 lb (15 419 kg); max payload, 14,508 lb (6 581 kg); max fuel, 12,830 lb (5 820 kg); max zero fuel, 48,500 lb (22 000 kg); max take-off, 54,010 lb (24 500 kg); max landing, 52,910 lb (24 000 kg).

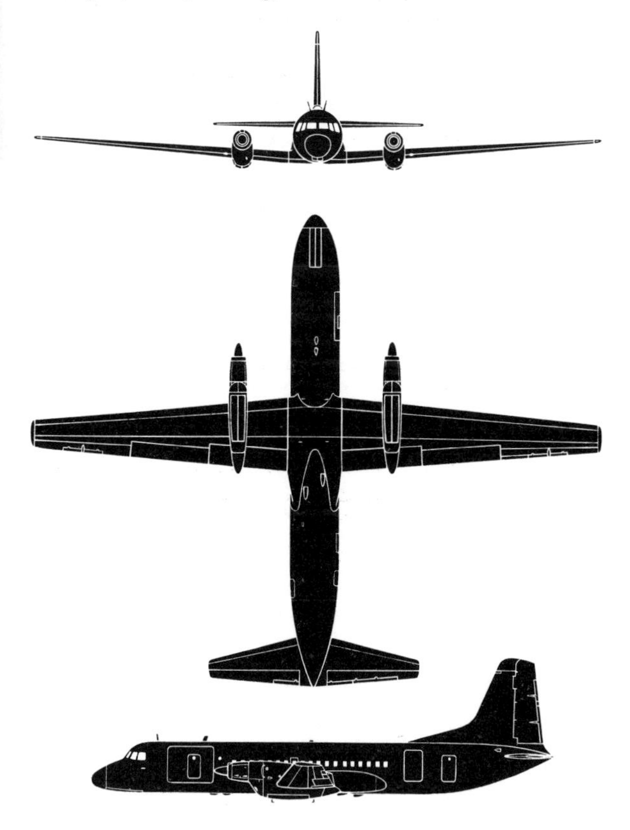

## PILATUS BRITTEN-NORMAN ISLANDER

**Country of Origin:** United Kingdom.
**Type:** Light general purpose transport.
**Power Plant:** Two 260 hp (194 kW) Lycoming O-540-E4C5 or 300 hp (224 kW) Lycoming IO-540-K1B5 piston engines.
**Performance** (IO-540 engines): Max cruise, 142 kts (264 km/h) at 7,000 ft (2 135 m); economical cruise, 132 kts (245 km/h); range, 555–613 naut mls (1 028–1 136 km) with standard fuel, 816–905 naut mls (1 513–1 677 km) with auxiliary fuel.
**Accommodation:** Pilot and up to nine passengers in pairs with no aisle.
**Status:** Prototype BN-2 flown 13 June 1965 with Continental IO-360 engines and 17 December 1965 with O-540 engines, second prototype flown 20 August 1966. First production Islander flown 24 April 1967; certification 10 August 1967 with first delivery 13 August (Glosair). First flown with IO-540 engines 30 April 1970 and with TIO-540 engines 30 April 1971. BN-2S (long-nosed) flown 22 August 1972. Turbo-Islander prototype (Lycoming LTP101 engines) flown 6 April 1977; BN-2T Turbine Islander (Allison 250 engines) flown 2 August 1980, certificated mid-1981, first deliveries 1982.
**Sales:** Nearly 1,100 Islanders of all variants (including military Defenders) sold by early 1987.
**Notes:** The Islander is used for a variety of tasks including air taxi and some scheduled services. Basic model has 260 hp (194 kW) piston engines and optional model has 300 hp (224 kW); both are available with extra fuel and extended wing tips. Turboprop version was introduced in 1981 and sales of this version continued following US certification on 15 July 1982.

## PILATUS BRITTEN-NORMAN ISLANDER

**Dimensions:** Span, 49 ft 0 in (14,94 m); span, fuel tanks in wing tips, 53 ft 0 in (16,15 m); length, 35 ft 7¾ in (10,87 m); height, 13 ft 8¾ in (4,18 m); wing area, 325.0 sq ft (30,19 m²); wing area, extended tips, 337.0 sq ft (31,31 m²).
**Weights:** Empty equipped, 3,738 lb (1 695 kg); max zero fuel weight, 6,300 lb (2 855 kg); max take-off and landing, 6,600 lb (2 993 kg).

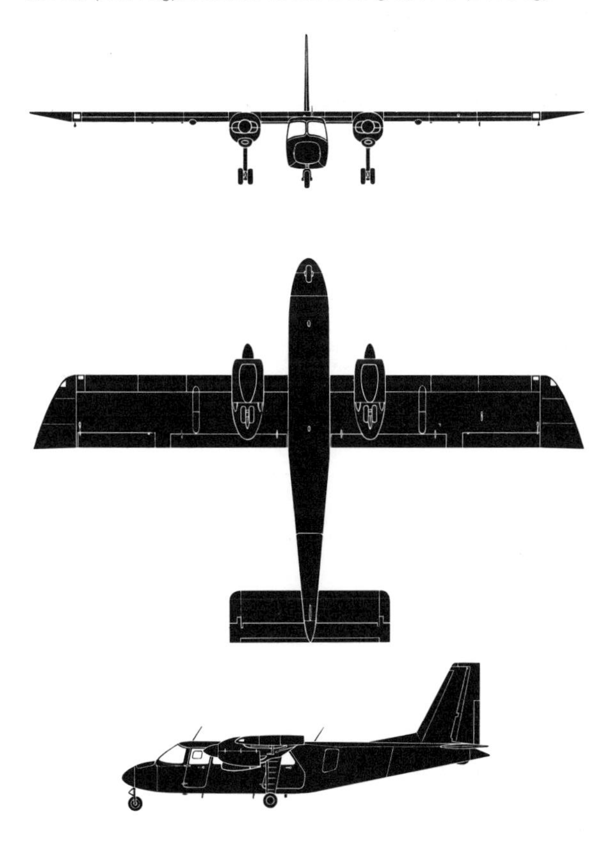

## PILATUS BRITTEN-NORMAN TRISLANDER

**Country of Origin:** United Kingdom.
**Type:** Commuter airliner and general utility transport.
**Power Plant:** Three 260 hp (194 kW) Avco Lycoming O-540-E4C5 piston engines.
**Performance** (BN2A Mk III-2): Max cruise, 144 kts (267 km/h) at 8,000 ft (2 438 m); long-range cruise, 130 kts (241 km/h) at 8,000 ft (2 438 m); max payload range (with 3,600 lb/1 633 kg payload, no reserves) 130 naut mls (241 km).
**Accommodation:** Flight crew of one or two and up to 17 passengers at 29-in (74-cm) pitch two-abreast with no aisle, access to seats through individual doors.
**Status:** Prototype first flown 11 September 1970; first production aircraft flown 6 March 1971 followed by certification on 14 May 1971. First customer delivery (Aurigny Air Services, Jersey) 29 June 1971.
**Sales:** Seventy-three Trislanders delivered and in service by end 1982. Production transferred to USA in 1982/83.
**Notes:** The Trislander originated as a three-engined, lengthened fuselage version of the Islander. It sold in only relatively small numbers (compared with more than 1,000 Islanders) and production in the UK was suspended in 1982, although the Trislander was still being actively promoted for the commuter market. In the USA, it is marketed by International Aviation Corporation as the Tri-Commutair; this company purchased eight completed aircraft and 12 sets of components to permit assembly of Tri-Commutairs at its plant near Miami, and IAC also has a licence for further Trislander/Tri-Commutair production if the market justifies such a step.

## PILATUS BRITTEN-NORMAN TRISLANDER

**Dimensions:** Span, 53 ft 0 in (16,15 m); length, 49 ft $2\frac{1}{2}$ in (15,00 m); height, 14 ft 2 in (4,32 m); wing area, 337 sq ft (31,30 $m^2$).
**Weights:** Operational empty, 5,843 lb (2 650 kg); max payload, 3,600 lb (1 633 kg); max zero fuel, 9,700 lb (4 400 kg); max take-off and landing, 10,000 lb (4 536 kg).

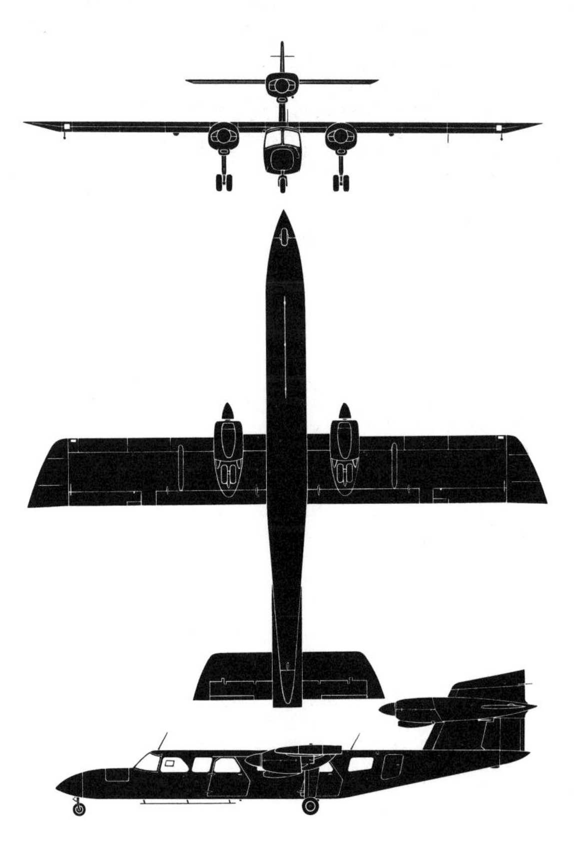

## PIPER T-1040 (AND CHIEFTAIN)

**Country of Origin:** USA.
**Type:** Light turboprop commuter liner.
**Power Plant:** Two 500 shp (373 kW) Pratt & Whitney PT6A-11 turboprops.
**Performance:** Max cruising speed, 236 kts (437 km/h) at 11,000 ft (3 355 m); long range cruise, 178 kts (330 km/h) at 10,000 ft (3 050 m); range with max payload, 590 naut mls (1 093 km); range with max fuel, 670 naut mls (1 241 km).
**Accommodation:** Eleven individual seats in cabin, including one or two pilot's seats side-by-side.
**Status:** Prototype T-1040 first flown 17 July 1981, certificated 25 February 1982; prototype T-1020 flown 25 September 1981. Deliveries began (T-1040) May 1982, (T-1020) December 1981.
**Sales:** Total of 22 T-1020 and 23 T-1040 delivered by 1986; production ended 1987. Some 500 Navajo Chieftains delivered for commuter use.
**Notes:** Piper Aircraft Corp set up an Airline Division in June 1981, and at the same time announced two new aircraft for commuter use. One, the T-1020, is essentially the same as the PA-31-350 Navajo Chieftain, several hundred of which were already in commuter operation (see photo); it has Lycoming IO-540 piston engines, a special interior to airline standards and reduced fuel capacity to permit a greater payload to be carried, including baggage in an extended nose compartment. The T-1040 (PA-31-T3) has basically the same fuselage as the T-1020, married to nose, wings and tail unit of the PA-31T-1 Cheyenne 1, including the latter's PT6A-11 turboprop engines. Several other Piper Twins are in commuter airline/air taxi use, including the T-tailed Cheyenne III and the smaller Aztec and Seneca.

## PIPER T-1040

**Dimensions:** Span, 41 ft 1 in (12,52 m); length, 36 ft 8 in (11,18 m); height, 13 ft 0 in (3,96 m); wing area, 229 sq ft (21,27 m²).

**Weights:** Operating weight empty, 4,624 lb (2 097 kg); fuel weight, 2,010 lb (912 kg); max payload, 2,976 lb (1 350 kg); max zero fuel, 7,600 lb (3 447 kg); max take-off and landing, 9,000 lb (4 082 kg).

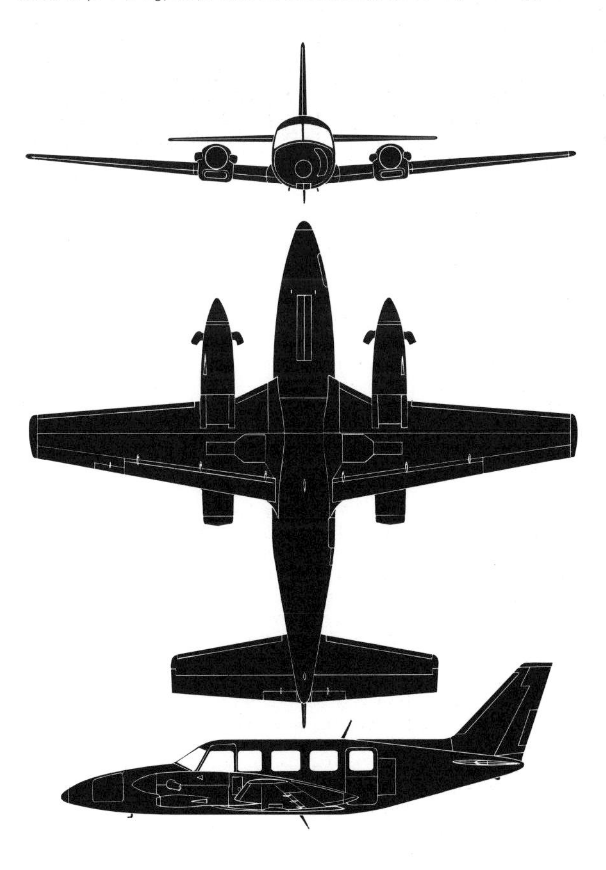

## SAAB SF-340

**Country of Origin:** Sweden and USA.
**Type:** Regional airliner.
**Power Plant:** Two 1,735 eshp (1 294 kW) General Electric CT7-5A2 turboprops.
**Performance:** Max cruise, 274 kts (508 km/h) at 15,000 ft (4 570 m); economical cruise, 252 kts (467 km/h) at 25,000 ft (7 620 m); range with 35-passenger payload, 500 naut mls (926 km).
**Accommodation:** Flight crew of two and 35 passengers at 30-in (76-cm) pitch three-abreast with offset aisle.
**Status:** First of two flying prototypes rolled out on 27 October 1982, with flight test commencing on 25 January 1983. Second and third aircraft flown on 11 May and 25 August 1983 respectively; first full production standard aircraft flown 5 March 1984. Certification 30 May 1984, first delivery (Crossair) 6 June.
**Sales:** Total of more than 90 sold by early 1987, of which about 70 delivered.
**Notes:** Saab-Scania (Sweden) and Fairchild Industries (USA) concluded an agreement on 25 January 1980, to develop the Model 340 regional airliner on a 50–50 basis. Fuselage construction and final assembly were undertaken in Sweden, with wings built by Fairchild at San Antonio; aircraft for North and Central America also were to be furnished and finished in the USA. At the end of 1985, Fairchild withdrew from the programme and Saab-Scania assumed full responsibility for marketing, with wing construction transferred to Sweden in 1987. Corporate and all-cargo versions have been developed.

## SAAB SF-340

**Dimensions:** Span, 70 ft 4 in (21,44 m); length, 64 ft 8 in (19,72 m); height, 22 ft 6 in (6,87 m); wing area, 450 sq ft (41,80 m²).
**Weights:** Operational empty, 17,215 lb (7 808 kg); max fuel, 5,690 lb (2 581 kg); max payload, 7,785 lb (3 581 kg); max take-off, 27,275 lb (12 371 kg); max landing, 26,500 lb (12 020 kg); max zero fuel, 25,000 lb (11 340 kg).

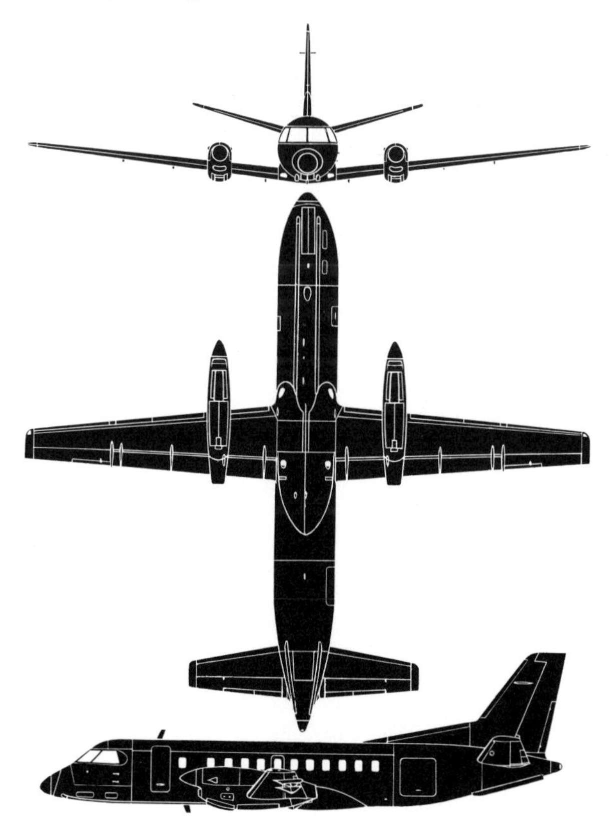

## SHORT BELFAST

**Country of Origin:** United Kingdom.
**Type:** Heavy duty freighter.
**Power Plant:** Four 5,730 shp (4 276 kW) Rolls-Royce Tyne RTy 12 turboprops.
**Performance:** Max cruise, 306 kts (566 km/h) at 24,000 ft (7 300 m); typical cruise, 275 kts (510 km/h); range with max payload, about 850 naut mls (1 575 km); range with 22,000-lb (10 000-kg) payload, 3,350 naut mls (6 200 km).
**Accommodation:** Flight crew of three or four. All-freight payload, with provision for up to 19 passengers on upper deck.
**Status:** First of 10 Belfast C Mk 1s for RAF flown 5 January 1964; deliveries began 20 January 1966. Certificated 6 March 1980 for commercial service starting same month.
**Sales:** Total of 10 aircraft built for RAF, in service until September 1976. five acquired ex-RAF by Eurolatin 1977 for civil conversion, of which three operated by TAC Heavylift (now Heavylift) with two in reserve in 1987.
**Notes:** The massive Belfast was developed to a specific RAF requirement for a long-range strategic freighter but was withdrawn from service after 10 years. For commercial operation by Heavylift (a subsidiary of the Trafalgar House group), Marshall of Cambridge designed and made a number of modifications to improve the low-speed control and to bring systems and equipment in general into line with contemporary civil standards. Of five aircraft available for conversion, three were in service by 1981, and have found a number of useful applications world-wide as a result of their large capacity with straight-in-loading through the rear door.

## SHORT BELFAST

**Dimensions:** Span, 158 ft 10 in (48,41 m); length, 136 ft 5 in (41,58 m); height, 47 ft 0 in (14,33 m); wing area, 2,466 sq ft (229,09 m²).

**Weights:** Typical operating weight empty, 130,000 lb (58 597 kg); max payload, 75,000 lb (34 000 kg); fuel load, 82,400 lb (37 376 kg); max zero fuel, 205,000 lb (92 986 kg); max take-off, 230,000 lb (104 325 kg), max landing, 215,000 lb (97 520 kg).

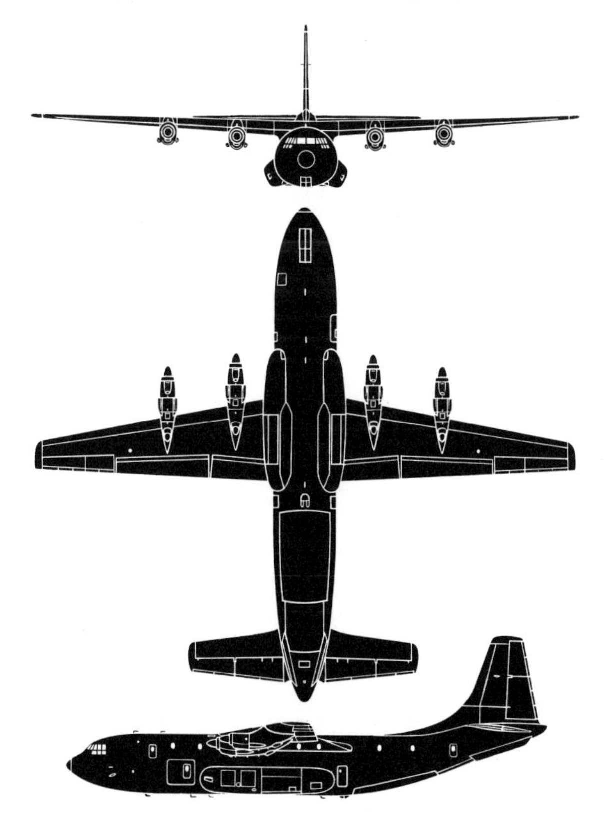

## SHORTS 330

**Country of Origin:** United Kingdom.
**Type:** Regional airliner.
**Power Plant:** Two (330–100) 1,173 shp (875 kW) Pratt & Whitney PT6A-45B or (330–200) 1,198 shp (893 kW) PT6A-45R turboprops.
**Performance** (330–200): Max cruise, 190 kts (352 km/h) at 10,000 ft (3 050 m); long-range cruise, 159 kts (294 km/h) at 10,000 ft (3 050 m); max payload range, (no reserves), 473 naut mls; range with max fuel, (no reserves) 915 naut mls (1 695 km).
**Accommodation:** Flight crew of two and 30 passengers at 30-in (76-cm) pitch three-abreast with offset aisle.
**Status:** Engineering prototypes (SD3-30) flown on 22 August 1974, with production prototype following on 8 July 1975. First production aircraft flown 15 December 1975, first customer deliveries mid-1976, entry into service (Time Air, Canada) 24 August 1976. The 330-200 was announced mid-1981.
**Sales:** More than 120 orders plus additional options had been placed for the Shorts 330 by beginning of 1987, for some two dozen operators, with nearly 100 aircraft delivered.
**Notes:** As the SD3-30, the Shorts 330 was evolved from the Skyvan, with same fuselage cross section but lengthened, and with greater wing span. Original gross weight was 22,690 lb (10 250 kg) with PT6A-45 engines. The 330-200 incorporates a number of product improvements, having similar engines to those of the 360 permitting elimination of the water-methanol system of the -100 and featuring as standard several items previously listed as options. The name Sherpa is used for a version with rear-loading door, first flown 23 December 1982.

## SHORTS 330

**Dimensions:** Span, 74 ft 8 in (22,76 m); length, 58 ft 0½ in (17,69 m); height, 16 ft 3 in (4,95 m); wing area, 453 sq ft (42,10 $m^2$).
**Weights** (330-200): Operational empty, 14,764 lb (6 697 kg); max payload (passenger), 5,850 lb (2 655 kg); max payload (freight), 7,500 lb (3 400 kg); max fuel, 4,480 lb (2 032 kg); max take-off, 22,900 lb (10 387 kg), max landing, 22,600 lb (10 251 kg).

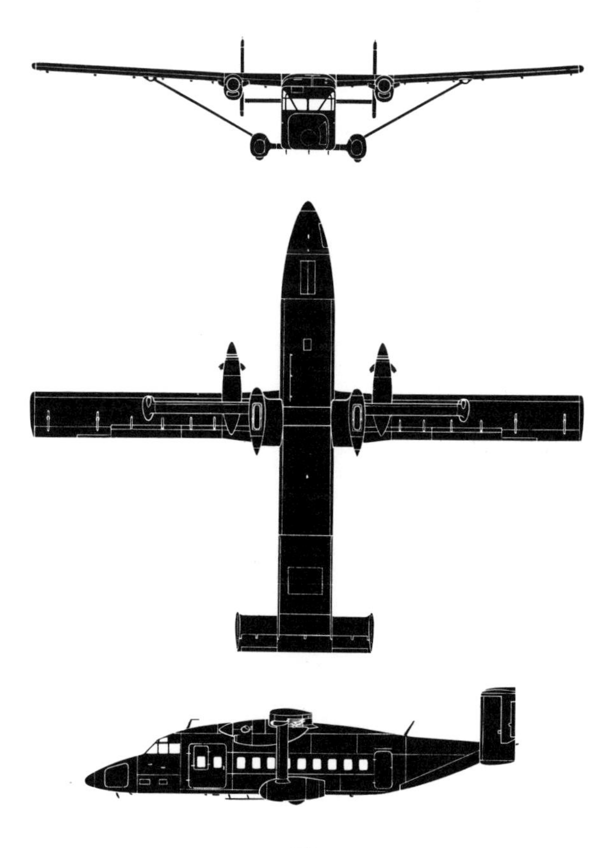

## SHORTS 360

**Country of Origin:** United Kingdom.
**Type:** Regional airliner.
**Power Plant:** Two flat-rated 1,424 shp (1 063 kW) Pratt & Whitney PT6A-65AR turboprops.
**Performance:** Max cruise, 212 kts (393 km/h) at 10,000 ft (3 050 m); long-range cruise, 180 kts (333 km/h) at 10,000 ft (3 050 m); max payload-range (36 passengers) (no reserves), 225 naut mls (417 km); range with max fuel, 861 naut mls (1 595 km).
**Accommodation:** Flight crew of two and 36 passengers at 30-in (76-cm) pitch three-abreast with offset aisle.
**Status:** Prototype first flown on 1 June 1981; first production 360 flown 19 August 1982 with certification on 3 September, and first customer delivery on 11 November 1982 (to Suburban Airlines of Pennsylvania) following US certification.
**Sales:** By beginning of 1987 orders and options totalled more than 120 aircraft from operators in three continents.
**Notes:** Essentially a growth version of the Shorts 330 (see previous page) the 360 differs from its progenitor primarily in having a 3-ft (91-cm) cabin stretch ahead of the wing and an entirely redesigned rear fuselage and tail assembly. These changes allow cabin capacity to be increased by two seat rows and result in lower aerodynamic drag which contributes to a higher performance. Like the 330, the 360 is unpressurized and is being produced alongside the earlier regional airliner, which remains somewhat less expensive. Early aircraft had lower-rated PT6A-65R engines, the PT6A-65AR being introduced in 1986 in the Shorts 360 Advanced.

## SHORTS 360

**Dimensions:** Span, 74 ft 10 in (22,81 m); length, 70 ft 10 in (21,59 m); height, 23 ft 8 in (7,21 m); wing area, 453 sq ft (42,10 m²).
**Weights:** Operational empty, 16,950 lb (7 688 kg); max fuel, 3,840 lb (1 741 kg); max payload, 7,020 lb (3 185 kg); max take-off, 26,000 lb (11 793 kg); max landing, 25,700 lb (11 657 kg).

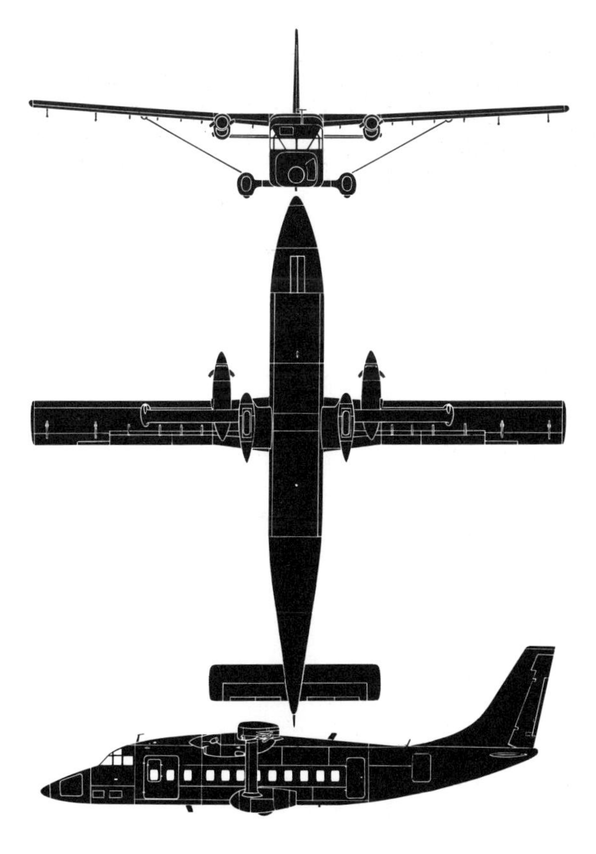

## TUPOLEV TU-134

**Country of Origin:** Soviet Union.
**Type:** Short/medium-range jetliner.
**Power Plant:** Two 14,990 lb st (6 800 kgp) Soloviev D-30 Srs II turbofans.
**Performance** (Tu-134A): Max cruise, 486 kts (898 km/h) at 28,000 ft (8 500 m); long-range cruise, 405 kts (750 km/h); range with max payload, 1,020 naut mls (1 890 km); range with payload of 11,025 lb (5 000 kg), 1,630 naut mls (3 020 km).
**Accommodation:** Flight crew of three (two pilots and a navigator). Max one-class layout, 84 passengers; typical mixed class accommodation, 12 plus 54, all four-abreast with central aisle.
**Status:** Prototype testing began late 1962, with five more aircraft flown 1963/64. Full commercial service began (with Aeroflot) September 1967 on Moscow–Stockholm route. Tu-134A entered service 1970.
**Sales:** More than 700 built for Aeroflot and for export to the East European airlines and Yugoslavia.
**Notes:** The Tu-134 emerged at about the same time as such Western types as the BAC One-Eleven and McDonnell Douglas DC-9, with which it shared a similar rear-engined T-tailed layout, and was the Tupolev design bureau's first wholly-original design for commercial use. The Tu-134A differs from the original model in having the fuselage lengthened by 6 ft 10$\frac{1}{2}$ in (2,10 m) and improved equipment. The Tu-134B has a forward-facing crew compartment. The Tu-134B-1 has a revised interior for up to 90 passengers (without a galley) and the Tu-134B-3 can seat 96 with full toilet and galley facilities retained. The Tu-134B-3 also makes use of the improved D-30-III turbofans.

## TUPOLEV TU-134A

**Dimensions:** Span, 95 ft $1\frac{3}{4}$ in (29,00 m); length, 121 ft $6\frac{1}{2}$ in (37,05 m); height, 30 ft 0 in (9,14 m); wing area, 1,370.3 sq ft (127,3 $m^2$).

**Weights:** Operating weight empty, 64,045 lb (29 050 kg); max payload, 18,075 lb (8 200 kg); max fuel weight, 31,800 lb (14 400 kg); max take-off, 103,600 lb (47 000 kg); max landing, 94,800 lb (43 000 kg).

## TUPOLEV TU-154

**Country of Origin:** Soviet Union.
**Type:** Medium-range jetliner.
**Power Plant:** Three (Tu-154) 20,950 lb st (9 500 kgp) Kuznetsov NK-8-2 or (Tu-154A and B) 23,150 lb st (10 500 kgp) NK-8-2U or (Tu-154M) 23,380 lb st (10 605 kgp) Soloviev D-30KU turbofans.
**Performance** (Tu-154M): Max cruising speed, 513 kts (950 km/h); economical cruising speed, 459 kts (850 km/h); range with max payload, 1,865 mls (3 000 km); range with 39,680-lb (18 000-kg) payload, 2,105 naut mls (3 900 km).
**Accommodation:** Normal flight crew of three (two pilots and flight engineer). Typical one-class layouts for 164 passengers six-abreast at 32-in (81-cm) pitch or 180 at 29.5-in (75-cm) pitch; mixed class layout for 8-24 first-class and 154 tourist class.
**Status:** First of six prototype/development Tu-154s flown on 4 October 1968. Early route-proving flights with Aeroflot began May 1971. First regular commercial service began within Soviet Union 9 February 1972 and first international service (Moscow–Prague) 1 August 1972. In production (Tu-154M) 1986.
**Sales:** More than 600 of all variants built for Aeroflot and for export to Balkan Bulgarian, Cubana, Malev, Tarom, LOT, Syrianair, Alyemda, Guyana Airways, CAAC and Choson Minhang.
**Notes:** The Tu-154 emerged in 1966, featuring a particularly good airfield performance and ability to operate from rough fields. The Tu-154A and Tu-154B are progressive improvements of the original Tu-154, and the Tu-154B-2 has imported French flight control and navaid equipment for Cat II operations. The Tu-154M introduces Soloviev D-30 engines.

## TUPOLEV TU-154M

**Dimensions:** Span, 123 ft $2\frac{1}{2}$ in (37,55 m); length, 157 ft $1\frac{3}{4}$ in (47,90 m); height, 37 ft $4\frac{3}{4}$ in (11,40 m); wing area, 2,169 sq ft (201,45 m$^2$).
**Weights:** Operating weight empty, 119,050 lb (54 000 kg); payload, 39,680 lb (18 000 kg); max fuel load, 87,633 lb (39 750 kg); max zero fuel weight, 163,150 lb (74 000 kg); max take-off, 220,460 lb (100 000 kg); max landing, 176,370 lb (80 000 kg).

## TUPOLEV TU-204

**Country of Origin:** Soviet Union.
**Type:** Medium-range turbofan transport.
**Power Plant:** Two 35,300 lb st (16 000 kgp) turbofans of unspecified type (believed to be Soloviev).
**Performance:** Max cruising speed, 459 kts (850 km/h) at 39,375 ft (12 000 m); best economy cruising speed, 437 kts (810 km/h) at 36,100 ft (11 000 m); range with 46,296-lb (21 000-kg) payload, 1,294 naut mls (2 400 km); range with 34,390-lb (15 600-kg) payload, 2,158 naut mls (4 000 km).
**Accommodation:** Flight crew of two (optionally three) and up to 214 passengers six-abreast with single aisle at 32-in (81-cm) pitch; typical mixed-class layout for 12 first-class, 11–47 'business'-class and 47–111 tourist-class, at seat pitches ranging from 39-in (99-cm) to 32-in (81-cm).
**Status:** Service entry expected by 1990.
**Sales:** None to date. Production for Aeroflot planned.
**Notes:** Completing the trio of jet and turboprop airliners under development for Aeroflot in the late 'eighties, the Tu-204 is in approximately the same category as the Boeing 757, and shares with that type the long, thin cabin with six-abreast seating and a single aisle. Expected to reach scheduled service use by the beginning of the 'nineties, the Tu-204 uses new engines, thought to have been developed by the Soloviev group bureau. It also has an advanced wing aerofoil section and advanced avionics and flying control system, with a four-tube EFIS-type presentation in the cockpit and the control sticks mounted off the instrument panel rather than the floor.

## TUPOLEV TU-204

**Dimensions:** Span, 137 ft 9½ in (42,00 m); length, 147 ft 7½ in (45,00 m).
**Weights:** Operating weight empty, 124,780 lb (56 600 kg); max payload, 48,500 lb (22 000 kg); max take-off, 207,230 lb (94 000 kg).

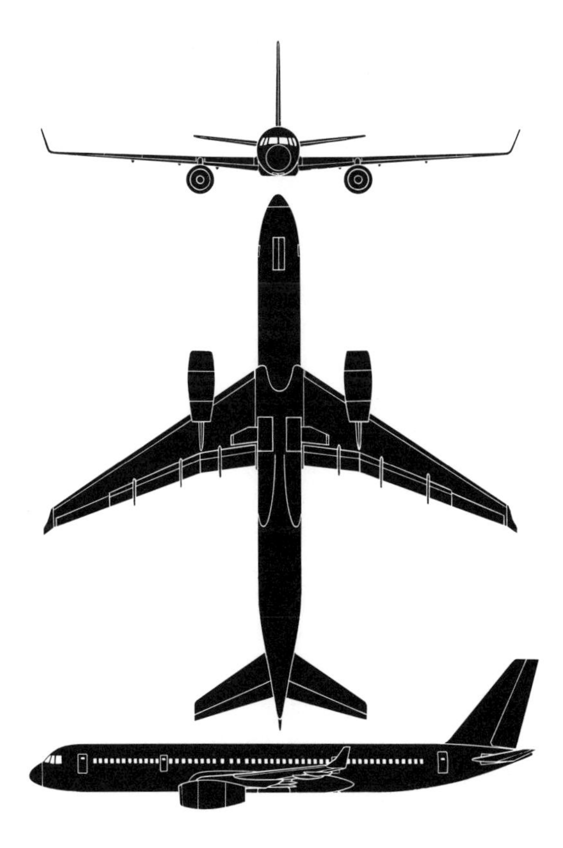

## VICKERS VANGUARD

**Country of Origin:** United Kingdom.
**Type:** Short- to medium-range turboprop airliner.
**Power Plant:** Four 5,545 eshp (4 135 kW) Rolls-Royce Tyne R Ty.11 Mk 512 turboprops.
**Performance:** High speed cruise, 369 kts (684 km/h) at 20,000 ft (6 100 m); long-range cruise, 365 kts (676 km/h) at 25,000 ft (7 620 m); range with max payload, 1,590 naut mls (2 945 km); range with max fuel and 20,000-lb (9 080-kg) payload, 2,693 naut mls (4 990 km).
**Accommodation:** Flight crew of two and up to 139 passengers at 34-in (86-cm) pitch, seated six-abreast with central aisle.
**Status:** Prototype (V-950) flown 20 January 1959; first production V.951 flown 22 April 1959; certificated 2 December 1960, entered service (BEA) 17 December 1960. First V.952 flown 21 May 1960, entered service (TCA) 1 February 1961. First V.953 flown 1 May 1961. First Merchantman flown 10 October 1969.
**Sales:** One prototype; six V.951 and 14 V.953 for BEA and 23 V.952 for TCA.
**Notes:** The Vanguard was evolved as an enlarged-capacity successor for the Viscount, but it was overtaken by the first of the short-haul pure jet transports and sales totalled only 43. Twelve of BEA's Vanguards were later converted to V-953C Merchantman standard with cargo loading door in forward fuselage side and cargo handling facilities. Vanguards sold by BEA and TCA (now Air Canada) were acquired by several smaller operators in Europe and Indonesia, and fewer than 10 of these remained in service by the end of 1986, primarily as freighters.

## VICKERS VANGUARD V.953

**Dimensions:** Span, 118 ft 7 in (36,15 m); length, 122 ft 10½ in (37,45 m); height, 34 ft 11 in (10,64 m); wing area, 1,529 sq ft (142,0 m²).
**Weights:** Empty equipped, 82,500 lb (37 422 kg); max payload, 37,000 lb (16 783 kg); max fuel load, 41,130 lb (18 656 kg); max zero fuel, 122,500 lb (55 564 kg); max take-off, 146,500 lb (66 448 kg); max landing, 130,500 lb (61 238 kg).

## VICKERS VISCOUNT

**Country of Origin:** United Kingdom.
**Type:** Short-range turboprop transport.
**Power Plant:** Four 2,100 ehp (1 566 kW) Rolls-Royce Dart 525 turboprops.
**Performance** (V.810): Typical cruising speed, 304 kts (563 km/h) at 20,000 ft (6 100 m); range with max (64-passenger) payload, 843 mls (1 560 km); range with max fuel, 877 naut mls (1 625 km).
**Accommodation:** Flight crew of two or three and up to 69 passengers five-abreast with off-set aisle, at 34-in (86-cm) pitch.
**Status:** V.630 prototype for Viscount series first flown 16 July 1948; V.700 flown 19 April 1950; first production V.701 flown 20 August 1952, certificated 17 April 1953 and entered service (BEA) 18 April. V.800 prototype flown 27 July 1956, first delivery (V.802 for BEA) 11 January 1957. V.810 prototype flown 23 December 1957. Production completed 1964.
**Sales:** Total of 438 Viscounts sold, plus six prototypes and unsold demonstrators. Major fleet buyers were BEA, TCA and Capital Airlines, About 40 Viscounts in airline service in 1987, plus others as executive transports.
**Notes:** The Viscount was the world's first turboprop airliner, entering service almost a year after the de Havilland Comet had become the world's first turbojet transport. The Viscount was also to prove the best-selling commercial transport of all-British design and production. The V.700 and V.800 variants differ in fuselage length, power and weights; individual customer variants within each series had identifying designations with '7' or '8' prefixes as appropriate.

## VICKERS VISCOUNT V.810

**Dimensions:** Span, 93 ft 8½ in (28,50 m); length, 85 ft 8 in (26,11 m); height, 26 ft 9 in (8,16 m); wing area, 963 sq ft (89,46 m²).

**Weights:** Basic operating, 41,565 lb (18 753 kg); max payload, 14,500 lb (6 577 kg); max fuel weight, 15,609 lb (7 080 kg); max zero fuel, 57,500 lb (26 082 kg); max take-off, 72,500 lb (32 886 kg); max landing, 62,000 lb (28 123 kg).

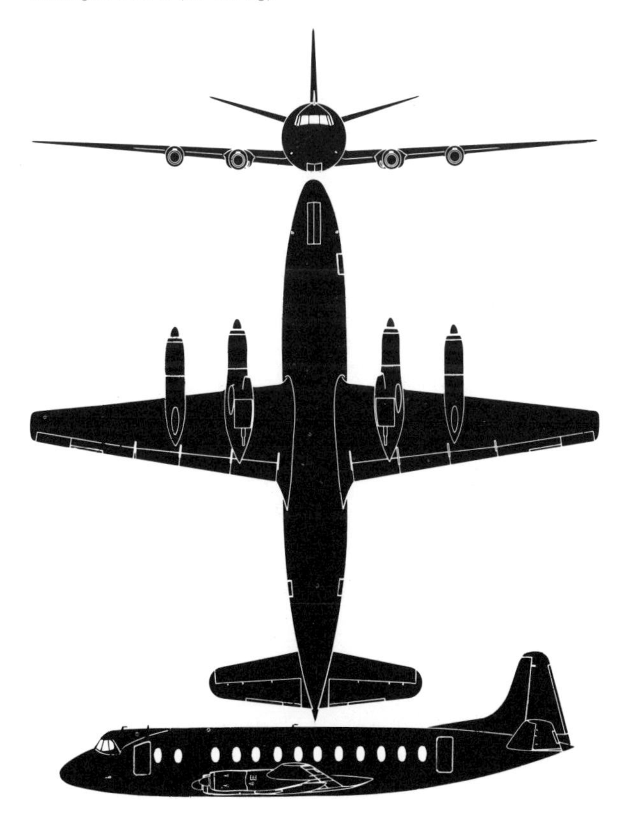

## XIAN Y7-100

**Country of Origin:** China.
**Type:** Short-to-medium range regional turboprop transport.
**Power Plant:** Two 2,550 shp (1 901 kW) Shanghai Wojiang WJ-5A-1 turboprops.
**Performance:** Max cruising speed, 261 kts (484 km/h) at 13,125 ft (4 000 m); long-range cruising speed, 228 kts (423 km/h) at 19,685 ft (6 000 m); range with full 52-passenger payload, 490 naut mls (910 km); range with standard fuel, 1,026 naut mls (1 900 km); range with max and auxiliary fuel, 1,305 naut mls (2 420 km).
**Accommodation:** Flight crew of three and up to 52 passengers four-abreast with central aisle.
**Status:** Prototype Y7-100 flown in Hong Kong autumn 1985. First production Y7-100 flown late 1986.
**Sales:** Total of 40 in production in 1987 for delivery to Chinese regional airlines.
**Notes:** After receiving a substantial number of Antonov An-24 transports from the Soviet Union, China has developed its own production drawings to allow manufacture of the type at the Xian factory. A pre-production example of the Chinese-built version, known as the Y7, was displayed in April 1982 and the first flight of a production Y7 was reported on 1 February 1984, with delivery to CAAC soon after. During 1985, Hong Kong Aircraft Engineering Co developed the Y7-100 featuring a revised and modernised cockpit, improved cabin, systems and avionics using Western equipment, and winglets. A Y7-200 variant is reported under development by Xian in 1986, with Boeing assistance and the Y7-300 designation refers to a version with a rear-loading ramp.

## XIAN Y7-100

**Dimensions:** Span, 97 ft 3 in (29,64 m); length, 77 ft 9 in (23,70 m); height, 28 ft 0½ in (8,55 m); wing area, 807.1 sq ft (74,98 $m^2$).
**Weights:** Operating weight empty, 32,850 lb (14 900 kg); max payload, 12,125 lb (5 500 kg); max fuel, 10,560 lb (4 790 kg); max take-off, 48,060 lb (21 800 kg); max landing, 48,060 lb (21 800 kg).

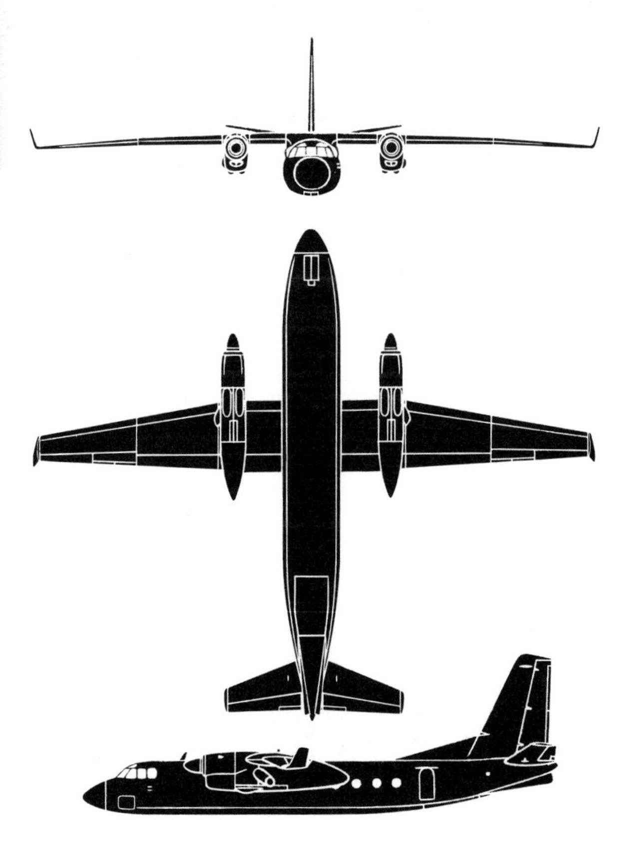

## YAKOVLEV YAK-40

**Country of Origin:** Soviet Union.
**Type:** Regional airliner.
**Power Plant:** Three 3,300 lb st (1 500 kgp) Ivchenko AI-25 turbofan engines.
**Performance:** Max cruising speed, 297 kts (550 km/h); range with max payload (32 passengers), 782 naut mls (1 450 km); range with max fuel, 971 naut mls (1 800 km).
**Accommodation:** Flight crew of two, with provision for third man on flight deck. Standard layout for 27 passengers three-abreast with offset aisle, at pitch of 29.7 in (77,5 cm); maximum high-density seating 32, four-abreast at same pitch.
**Status:** Prototype first flown 21 October 1966. Entered service with Aeroflot 30 September 1968. Production (commercial and military) complete.
**Sales:** Approximately 1,000 built, principally for use by Aeroflot. Some exports to companies or governments in Italy, Federal Germany, Afghanistan, Angola, Czechoslovakia, Bulgaria, Vietnam, and Yugoslavia.
**Notes:** Yakovlev's first jet transport, the Yak-40 was designed to meet Soviet needs for a short-haul transport of modest capacity, to replace piston-engined Il-12s and Il-14s, and even older Li-2s. It flies on scheduled services but is also used for ambulance and air taxi duties and several have been supplied for military use. An effort was also made to adapt the Yak-40 for the US commuter airline market, by fitting Garrett TFE731 turbofans and Collins avionics; this programme was handled by ICX Aviation as the X-Avia, but it did not proceed. An all-freight version of the Yak-40 is used in the Soviet Union, where about 700 are believed to be still in service in 1987.

## YAKOVLEV YAK-40

**Dimensions:** Span, 82 ft 0¼ in (25,00 m); length, 66 ft 9½ in (20,36 m); height, 21 ft 4 in (6,50 m); wing area, 735.5 sq ft (70,0 $m^2$).
**Weights:** Empty weight, 20,725 lb (9 400 kg); max payload, 5,070 lb (2 300 kg); max fuel load, 8,820 lb (4 000 kg); max take-off weight, 35,275 lb (16 000 kg).

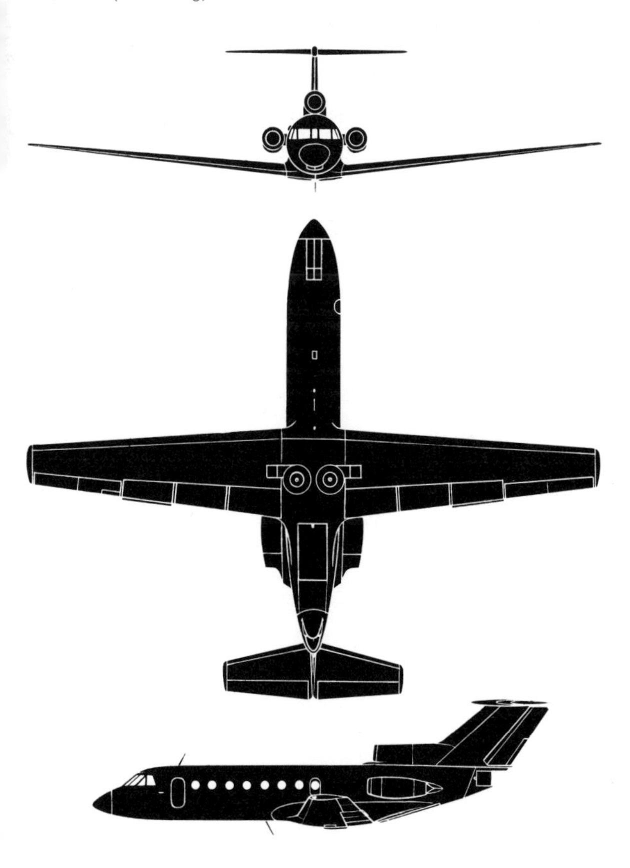

## YAKOVLEV YAK-42

**Country of Origin:** Soviet Union.
**Type:** Short/medium-range jetliner.
**Power Plant:** Three 14,330 lb st (6 500 kgp) Lotarev D-36 turbofan engines.
**Performance:** Max cruising speed, 437 kts (810 km/h) at 25,000 ft (7 600 m); best economy cruise, 405 kts (750 km/h); range with payload of 23,810 lb (10 800 kg), 940 naut mls (1 740 km); range with max fuel, 2,050 naut mls (3 800 km).
**Accommodation:** Flight crew of two. Standard arrangement for 120 passengers six-abreast with central aisle, at 29.5 in (75 cm) pitch.
**Status:** First of three prototypes flown 7 March 1975. First production aircraft flown 1980, and Aeroflot services began at the end of that year, on Moscow–Krasnodar route.
**Sales:** About 50 delivered to Aeroflot by 1986.
**Notes:** The Yak-42 is an extrapolation of the Yak-40 design, and was regarded by Aeroflot as one of the most important additions to its fleet, primarily for domestic routes. First prototype had only 11 deg of sweepback on the wing, increased to 23 deg on the two subsequent prototypes and production aircraft, which also introduced four-wheel main landing gear bogies in place of twin wheels. Yak-42 services were withdrawn in 1982, apparently after difficulties were encountered with the early aircraft, and reintroduced in 1984. The Yak-42M has a lengthened fuselage and 16,550 lb (7 500 kgp) Lotarev D-436 engines. Expected to enter Aeroflot service in 1987, it can accommodate up to 168 passengers and has improved equipment. With a gross weight of 145,500 lb (66 000 kg), its range is 1,350 naut mls (2 500 km) with max payload and 2,160 naut mls (4 000 km) with max fuel.

## YAKOVLEV YAK-42

**Dimensions:** Span, 114 ft 5¼in (34,88 m); length, 119 ft 4¼ in (36,38 m); height, 32 ft 3 in (9,83 m); wing area, 1,615 sq ft (150 m²).
**Weights:** Empty equipped, 71,650 lb (32 500 kg); max payload, 30,865 lb (14 000 kg); max fuel load, 40,785 lb (18 500 kg); max take-off, 119,050 lb (54 000 kg); max landing, 110,230 lb (50 000 kg).

# INDEX